HIT HARD AND ENJOY IT

by

T. C. 'Dickie' Dodds

with a preface by Sir Neville Cardus

*'In all the annals of cricket there
has been no player with so remarkable
and inspiring a story to tell.'*

Sir Neville Cardus

First published 1976 by
The Cricketer Ltd.,
Beech Hanger, Ashurst, Tunbridge Wells, Kent, England.

ISBN 0 902211 04 8
Paperback edition: ISBN 0 902211 05 6

EDITOR: DAVID FRITH

Printed by John G. Eccles, Inverness, Scotland

Contents

Preface by Sir Neville Cardus

Introduction

To
Ann and Michael

Preface

by Sir Neville Cardus

In an age when the media need to create more or less glamorous and
fictitious personalities, many a genuine character of individuality
and skill is overlooked or provides only a ten days' wonder. I am
pleased to write the preface for this book; and I hope that before the
reader has gone through it — and I hope that before he has gone
through this preface — he will realise that T. Carter ('Dickie')
Dodds is a man to be marked out of thousands. He learned to play
cricket on the lawn of his father's vicarage; he was indeed son of a
clergyman. He learned the game with his three brothers. On wet
days the boys played in a yard with a wall which prevented strokes
to the off side, so to score profitably the young batsmen needed to
pull or hook. In the course of time 'Dickie' developed into an
intrepid, powerful hooker; at his best he would, I fancy, have coped
joyously with the Australian Thomson.

He was educated at Wellingborough and Warwick Schools,
leaving at the age of sixteen. He was baptised in organised cricket by
appearing anonymously (as far as performance was concerned) in
the Warwickshire and Middlesex second elevens, round about 1937
and 1939. He served with the Army, 1939 to 1945, and played for
a Services XI captained by D. R. Jardine, in Bombay, against India.
He scored 14, taking an afternoon to collect these runs. As a fact,
he for a long time batted against his nature, for clergyman father
despite, he lived well, savouring the good things of the world earthy
and fleshy. It was as a leg-break bowler that he was introduced to
the Essex county XI; but, determined to establish himself as a
first-class professional cricketer, he schooled himself to bat safely
and solidly, resisting the sinful temptations presented by half-volleys

and long hops. Then happened the transformation, the conversion. On the morning of his first game for Essex he, in his own words, 'asked God how I should play cricket' — against Sussex at Ilford, on May 22, 1946 — and the clear thought came: 'Hit the ball hard and enjoy it.' But he could not obey the advice of Omnipotence immediately. Though he scored 63 in this baptism match against Sussex, he continued to inhibit himself for two and a half hours.

After earning his county cap following a record opening partnership of 270, with A. V. Avery at The Oval, he decided to obey the God-sent injunction 'to hit the ball'. In a day, 'Dickie' became miraculously transfigured — there's no other word for it. Against Middlesex at Westcliff, he drove, cut and hooked with an easy power and brilliance which astounded everybody. Still, even now, old doubts, backslidings of faith, visited him. Against Hampshire he 'hit the ball' until his score had arrived at 98; then, to himself, he said warningly, 'Go steady for your century.' His innings became becalmed, immobile, false. 'I could not understand what had happened,' he relates, 'then I remembered — I had said ''No'' to God, and taken up my old material safety-first philosophy. I threw it all out, hit the next ball over mid-off for four, and that was that.'

For the rest of his career, as cricketer, his rate of scoring was 40 runs every hour. And from 1946 to 1956 his total of runs was 16,710, average 29.98. In 1947 his aggregate of runs was 2147, average 38. One day, against Lancashire, he hit the first two balls from Statham for four and six. At last he was fulfilled, true to himself, the Beau Sabreur of the cricket of his period. We have seen little like it, in English cricket, since Dexter laid down his bat, all too soon.

It was in 1946 that 'Dickie', after long spiritual questionings, decided to give his mind, faith and material aid to the Moral Re-Armament movement, 'as an experiment to see if God could make clear His will for me, and direct every area of my life, and show how a better world could be created.' In 1957, Essex granted 'Dickie' a benefit match, which enriched him by £2300. During the crowded game a small boy asked 'Dickie', 'What are you going to do with all that money?' And 'Dickie' replied, 'I am going to help to build a new world.' Whereat the small boy, rightly and expressively, said, 'Cor!' Dodds gave all his benefit money to Moral Re-Armament.

It is possible that opponents of Essex County Cricket Club might have protested had they known that God was aiding 'Dickie' as he hooked and cut and drove the bowling, the Puritan wearing the bright colours of the Happy Cavalier. I am reminded that at the turn of the century another religious-minded professional cricketer played for Leicestershire, named A. E. Knight. He always came in to bat second-wicket-down. After taking guard, he would close his eyes, head down, in prayer. One day Leicestershire were playing Lancashire, and Lancashire's fast bowler, the gusty amateur, Walter Brearley, had taken two quick wickets when Knight appeared at the crease, asking the umpire for 'two leg', then closing his eyes. Brearley was perplexed, and hoarsely whispered to mid-off, 'What's the matter with him, is he ill?' 'No,' whispered back mid-off, 'he's praying.' 'Praying? What's he praying for?' 'Well,' whispered mid-off, 'I suppose he's praying for God to get him a century.' 'What?' roared Brearley, 'I'll write to the MCC about this!'

But 'Dickie' did not openly display his devotions. As I say, he was, after conversion, a Beau Sabreur, chivalrous, caring, playing with a 'glorious uncertainty', a prematurely-greyhaired young 'Dickie' who, like Peter Pan, wouldn't grow up.

In all the annals of cricket there has been no player with so remarkable and inspiring a story to tell. I have met him and have felt the influence of his belief. Not that he has argued about religion, or advocated it with and to me. I myself have tried hard to find God, called on Him, and had no answer. I am as impatient with the dogmatism of an atheist as I am with the dogmatism of an archbishop. For me, creation is a mystery. A God I could identify personally would belittle this mystery. Whether 'Dickie' has found God or has only consolidated faith cannot rationally be proven, as far as I see it. The great thing is that he had found and incorporated to himself — goodness. That is why I admire him, and why I have written this preface to his book.

Introduction

This book was Sir Neville Cardus's idea. And without his persistence it would never have been written.

During my playing career I knew Sir Neville as a legendary writer on cricket but it was not until I retired from the game that I got to know him as a man. We often met at Lord's, and there over the seasons we would talk cricket.

One day, in the Lord's pavilion, he broached a quite different subject. 'Dickie,' he said, 'you've got a faith. I can see you've got a faith. How did you get it?'

As I told him my story he kept interrupting, saying, 'It's got to be a book.'

When I had finished he said, 'It's like letting half volley after half volley go by and not hitting them. You must write all this in a book.'

I told Sir Neville I had no idea how to go about such a task. 'You can do it,' he said. 'Just write it down as you talk. Write for an hour a day. At the end of the week you will have so many words. At the end of a month so many. Don't make it long. There are too many long books. Now promise me you'll do it and I'll promise to write the preface.'

A few days later I started my hour a day. At the end of two months I had written twenty thousand words. Then I got stuck and remained stuck.

The first thing Sir Neville said to me when I saw him at Lord's the next summer was, 'How is the book coming?' I told him I was stuck. 'Oh never mind about that,' he said. 'I often get stuck. The thing is to leave it awhile and then take it out and look at it afresh.'

I followed his recipe and delivered the finished typescript to him just before Christmas, wrapped in festive paper.

He was delighted it was completed. When he had fulfilled his side of the bargain, he rang up. 'Come and have lunch and I'll read it to you.'

I met him at a restaurant near his flat where he often ate. He was already at his usual table. Even before we had ordered he produced his manuscript, written in his beautifully clear hand. He read it out to me, and to all within earshot, in a loud declamatory voice, chuckling hugely at the parts he especially liked.

We had a merry lunch. We talked cricket of course. He also spoke of some of the deepest things on his heart: his gratitude for the great good fortune he felt he had had in his life, his beliefs, and his lack of faith. He always liked to insist he had no faith.

Then the next moment he would tell me what seemed at variance with this. For instance, how he took Bertrand Russell to task for his disbelief in God, asking him how he, as an intelligent man, could possibly believe that the wonder of the world had come about by chance. He would also tell how he had once expressed his ritual doubts to Archbishop Temple, for whom he had a great regard. The Archbishop replied, 'Neville — I only wish I had a curate with as much faith as you. It's just that you call it something different.'

Sir Neville said over lunch how much he would like to get down on his knees and thank someone for all the good things he had had in his life — for his tremendous gratitude. 'But,' he said, 'I don't know whom to thank.' I took my courage in both hands and said, 'Neville, I know from your books that you never met your earthly father nor even knew who he was. Do you think your unwillingness to acknowledge your Heavenly Father could somehow spring from this?' His eyes seemed to travel down the mists of time. 'Yes,' he murmured, 'it may.' He went on to tell me something of the hurts of those early years.

When I rang him the following day, I thanked him for the lunch and preface and then asked if any illumination had come on the subject we had touched on at the end of our meal. He said it hadn't, though he thought he could see some light at the end of the tunnel.

Then he turned to this book. One of his themes with me had been his puzzlement at the boredom with life of some of the younger people he met. He could not understand it, especially since they had opportunities for which he, at their age, would have given his eye teeth. To him, at 85, life was still full of interest, fun, adventure, and above all a fascinating mystery. 'That is why your book is important,' he said. 'People must read it. It will help.'

His last words to me were, 'You know, I think I am more keen on this book than you are.'

A week later, on February 28, 1975, I turned on the radio to listen to the early morning news and heard that Neville Cardus had died peacefully in his sleep. The preface must be the last thing he wrote.

So here is the story he got me to write. It is told in the setting of the work of a run-of-the-mill cricketer, the week-in-week-out county round. But first I must tell a little about my life before entering first-class cricket, for it is the way in which my re-discovery of God affected my game which Sir Neville most wanted me to describe. While my love of cricket began, as he says, in my father's vicarage garden, faith became a working reality rather than a formality or an irritant during my time in the Army and immediately afterwards. So, if I am to fulfil my commission, a little autobiography is unavoidable.

CHAPTER 1

Opening My Innings

My innings began in Bedford on May 29, 1919. My mother had gone to a nursing home there for my birth. As soon as she and I were able to travel, we went by pony and trap over the country lanes to the village of Riseley, ten miles away, where my father was vicar. There we were greeted by a special peal on the church bells.

What could be better than to start life in the Bedfordshire countryside in June? There are no lanes or fields I love more than those around Riseley. Others may be more beautiful, but none have the same power to tug at my heartstrings. Perhaps it is a universal experience that wherever we spend our earliest days stirs the deepest places in our being.

The big, rambling vicarage was surrounded by lawns and ponds, outbuildings and stables. There was a tennis court on one side of the house, and a lawn with cricket nets on the other. If you hit a ball back over the bowler's head, it would sail across a yew hedge into the churchyard. And when you went to look for it, you might discover, in the shelter of a sloping tombstone, a partridge sitting on its olive-green eggs.

Father worked hard. One parishioner said he never saw him walking from house to house on his calls, only running. He looked after more than one parish. On Sunday mornings, after his sermon in Riseley church, he would announce the last hymn and leave by pony and trap for the neighbouring village, arriving just in time to preach again.

He was a native of Oxford. His father, a Doctor of Music, was the organist at Queen's College for many years and father graduated there after school in Oxford. He used to know William Morris, who kept a nearby cycle shop, and they wrote to each other from time to time till the end of Lord Nuffield's life. When father was at Oxford, sport was thought as important a part of University life as study, and cricket was his love. He bowled right-arm at medium pace and left-arm slow. I have never known anyone bowl with both arms with such skill.

Father's salary as vicar of Riseley was £199 a year. Even in those days this was not much, and he soon had four sons to feed. Despite this, we kept a cook, a maid, and a gardener. To earn more money, father took in students from overseas, coaching them for entrance examinations to colleges and universities.

My earliest memories are of excelling at cricket. Our gardener, Wilfred Gell, was the village fast bowler. I don't know what he was like as a gardener but he could certainly bowl, and because of my father's keenness on cricket he knew he could always safely leave the vegetable patch and bowl to me. On Sunday, Wilfred kept his bowling muscles in trim by pumping the church organ.

My mother came from Leeds. She was of Quaker stock. The position of vicar's wife meant a new sort of life for her. But she learnt well and became a superb cook and household organiser as well as doing her duties in the parish.

When I was nine my father moved to the parish of Wymington in Northamptonshire and I began as a day boy in the junior section of Wellingborough School. This small public school had as its head-master P. A. Fryer, who seemed to have his priorities clear: first cricket, second football, third athletics, fourth study.

I loved Wellingborough. The playing fields were magnificent, and games were played with gusto. I soon made my way as a cricketer, both in our spare-time games in the schoolyard, and in organised matches.

One day two of us were bowling and batting to each other after lunch, our coats heaped on the grass as wickets. Unknown to us, the master in charge of junior school cricket was watching. After a while he called to me, 'What's your name?' I told him. 'Well, Dodds, you bowl a very good length.' At that time I could not have said what a good length was but I felt as if I had been given a knighthood. I was soon playing for the junior school team as a batsman and bowler.

Every aspect of the game was dealt with at Wellingborough. Boys were taught to 'break in' a new bat with as meticulous care as a musician a violin. The new blade would be carefully oiled. A cricket ball that had grown soft with use would be bounced gently up and down it. The ball would then be put in an old sock and swung again and again onto the blade. Finally, after several hours of this treatment, the boy would take his bat and begin to hit the ball into the side of a cricket net, starting gently and only after some days actually driving the ball. All this was amply repaid by the driving power and lasting qualities of the bat.

We also had to roll our own pitches. I have always been grateful for the experience. Every cricketer ought to know how to prepare a good pitch.

During this time I had my first cricket accident. It happened when two of us ran to catch the same ball and met head to head. I had a bad blow and for a while suffered painful headaches; so painful that they almost extinguished my passion for the game.

I spent four happy years at Wellingborough. Then my father was offered the parish of Hatton in Warwickshire. I was given the choice of staying on at Wellingborough as a boarder or going to Warwick School as a day boy. I chose Warwick.

I was soon in the cricket first eleven. I can still see the look of curiosity on the faces of my team-mates as we left by train for our first away match and the master in charge bought full-fare tickets for the others and a half-fare for me.

Our cricket captain that year was A. G. K. Brown, who ran with electric speed and won a silver medal for Britain in the Olympic Games in 1936 in the 400 metres event. He was our fast bowler. I would not say he had the classical fast bowler's action. He sprinted up to the wicket and then just seemed to let the ball carry on. His running was like poetry. We could not imagine him ever beaten. We were numb with disbelief when the news came through that he had been headed into second place in the Games.

I became the opening bat for the school and was a change bowler at medium pace. In the nets I also bowled leg-breaks. I had learned to do this at an early age while bowling underarm in miniature cricket matches played in confined spaces. It is an ideal way to learn this sort of spin bowling because the action for spinning the ball is the same whether underarm or overarm. The googly too.

One summer I had an accident which considerably affected my cricket. I was hit quite badly on the head while batting. Coming to on the pitch and being unable to get up was an extremely unpleasant experience. I had concussion. Nevertheless I played for the school the following Saturday. I was hit on the head again. This was at an away match and there was the agony of the jolting bus trip back with a splitting headache.

For some time after this I tended to wince whenever I heard a ball on a bat, and my relish for batting vanished to such an extent that I thought I had better concentrate on bowling from now on.

About this time I read a book by the great Australian spin bowler, Clarrie Grimmett, and decided to try his recipe for success. He had spent years practising with six balls in his garden, bowling at a mark on the pitch to perfect length. He had a dog to bring the balls back. I had no dog, but I got six balls and bowled at my mark.

One of the teams that played against Warwick School was the Warwickshire Club and Ground side. I secretly hoped that I would catch the eye of the Warwickshire authorities during these games and that they would invite me for a trial with the county. They showed not the slightest interest.

By the time I reached seventeen I had no idea what I wanted to do with my life. I had never known. I envied those who with such certainty felt called to be doctors or lawyers and who went steadily ahead to their objective. I had no desire to make money nor incentive to study. My school reports were always: 'Could do better if he tried.' What I wanted to know was to what end should I try?

So at seventeen, with no exams passed or in prospect of being passed, I was told by the headmaster that he thought the best thing for me was to leave. I thought so too. For one thing, it would make it easier for my brothers' fees to be paid.

Through a parishioner, my father arranged for me to join an insurance firm. But before I could start, a routine medical examination was required and this I failed. My own doctor confirmed that I had a bad chest and heart and sent me to bed for six months.

When I got up in the spring, pronounced fit, an uncle, building a telephone exchange in Oxford, took me on. So I moved into lodgings in the city of my forbears.

The telephone exchange was on Boars Hill. I brewed the tea and generally tried to make myself useful; I suspect without much success. I also joined the North Oxford Cricket Club and had considerable success. I made a lot of runs.

One day a telegram arrived which altered my whole life. It was an invitation from Warwickshire to have a trial with them for the remainder of the summer, starting immediately. Apparently news of my exploits in Oxford had reached them. I travelled in a daze of heady delight at the prospect which I thought lay ahead.

CHAPTER 2

Saturday Cricketer

I packed my bag with great care before my first match. It was against Northamptonshire second eleven. I arrived at the ground in a nervous state, which was made worse by my going into the professionals' room and being told I must go to the amateurs' room next door.

Then I found I had left behind my white socks. It seemed like the end of the world. I hesitantly explained the position to our captain and asked if he could lend me a pair. He laughed and said it didn't matter, I could use the dark ones I had on. He was making pleasantries in the pros' room at the time, and as I went out I heard him say, 'There's one player who's got the wind up.'

Worse was to follow. We batted first, and when my turn came I snicked the third or fourth ball on to my pads and was given out, leg-before-wicket. I was making my miserable way towards the pavilion when I heard someone running up behind. It was the fielding captain. 'I'm sorry you were given out,' he said. 'We would like you to come back.'

This generosity to a beginner made me even more embarrassed. A few balls later I was bowled.

They say even a worm will turn, and I was so mad by the time we had to field that I tore after every ball that came near. The captain, whom I had begun to hate, re-instated himself in my esteem by congratulating me on my fielding.

I played for Warwickshire second eleven for the rest of that summer but had only mediocre success. When autumn came I looked for a winter job. An advertisement for an assistant in the office of the Amateur Football Alliance in London caught my eye. I wrote off and got the job.

The AFA had an office near London Bridge, run by Capt. W. G. Greenland. He sat on one side of a desk, and I the other, and we were it. My task was to make sure that all games run by the AFA had a referee and linesmen, and to send out the cards telling these gentlemen where to officiate.

When spring came, I expected to go back to cricket. But I got a letter from the Warwickshire secretary saying that in their opinion I was not strong enough for three-day cricket. They were no longer interested in my services.

Capt. Greenland was most solicitous. I got a job with a printing firm, but two weeks later was approached by Barclays Bank. Greenland had passed the word that his former assistant was a promising cricketer — a possible addition to the bank side. I took the job with Barclays.

In 1938 Barclays had a very strong side captained by R. N. 'Nobby' Hunt, a fine cricketer who had played for Middlesex. In those days junior clerks, even those playing for the bank first eleven, had a long morning's slog in the office on a Saturday and were always the last to leave.

When I got to the ground for my first match, it had been in progress for some time. I changed, ran onto the field, was put in the slips, and very first ball hung on to a high flier.

It was the luck of the game, for this beginning put me in the good books of 'Nobby' Hunt. From that day he was my faithful friend and adviser. 'Nobby' Hunt lived for cricket. He played it hard and I enjoyed playing under him. We seemed to win most of our matches and my recollection is that we were the best club side in London.

Hunt decided I would best serve the team as a leg-break bowler. He thought spin bowlers needed to have their fingers sensitive and supple, and that batting tended to blunt their 'feel'. So he put me low down in the batting order.

Whenever I did well, Capt. Greenland, who wrote a cricket column in a London evening paper, would feature his late assistant's success, once concluding with the remark that surely Middlesex could not afford much longer to ignore this talented young cricketer!

I was not good at banking. My job was to sit on a high stool and enter something called 'waste' into a large ledger. I cannot remember what 'waste' was. At the end of the day I had to add up the long columns of figures I had written down. I could seldom get the same answer twice.

I also had to copy the manager's letters. He wrote these in a special ink. I then put them in a large press with a piece of damp tissue paper over each. I screwed the press down and, if I got the pressure right, and hadn't used too much water in the damping process, a copy of the letter came off on the tissue. The scope for error was great and, during the period when I operated this piece of technology, many were the letters that had to be re-written by the manager.

It was not surprising that the manager called me into his office for a serious talk. He said that unless there was a very marked improvement in my work, my services would be dispensed with. Something exploded inside me. I was damned if I was going to be thrown out of a bank. If I went, I would go of my own accord and in my own time. I learned to copy the letters and add up the figures.

I had little money. The bank paid me £60 a year and father managed to send me ten shillings a week. After paying for my lodgings and fares and a daily lunch of a glass of milk and an orange, I had two shillings a week left over. In the winter I spent this watching Arsenal playing football one week, and the Harringay Greyhounds playing ice hockey the next. Arsenal were then the most famous football club in the world. Their crowds were immense.

One Saturday, at half-time, I was surprised to see the Arsenal manager come onto the field with some of the most prominent sportsmen of the day. Two I remember were 'Bunny' Austin, the tennis player, and George Eyston, the racing driver. A microphone was produced, and these gentlemen proceeded to talk to the crowd about Moral Re-Armament. I was momentarily impressed that men like these should talk on such a subject at a football match.

On summer afternoons in London, I would scan the paper to see if Denis Compton was likely to be batting at Lord's. If he was, I would spend my two bob on the chance of seeing him in action. Denis was for me the most exciting cricketer of them all. Little did I dream that he would make a century — and before lunch at that — in my own benefit match nineteen years later.

Eventually, in the summer of 1939, I had an invitation to play for Middlesex second eleven. These were two-day matches, the time for which I had to take out of my holiday.

I continued to play for Middlesex for the remainder of the season but did so poorly that, by the time the last game, v. Surrey, came, I decided that cricket was not the career for me. Then in the second innings I took six wickets. Hope returned. In the Surrey side were huge twins called Bedser.

During this final game the barrage balloons were already flying overhead.

CHAPTER 3

Hitler Interrupts

During my time in London I observed the nation bumbling on to war with growing fury and frustration. My feelings were mirrored in a book called *Guilty Men* written shortly after the war began. I was outside 10 Downing Street when war was actually declared.

A few days later I joined up. The only exam I had passed at school was in the Officers Training Corps, and so I went along with my Certificate A to the recruiting centre at the Inns of Court Regiment in the City to answer the call for 'potential officers'. To my surprise and relief a medical board passed me A1. I soon received my posting, which was to the Somerset Light Infantry at Jelalabad Barracks, Taunton.

By the strangest of coincidences the same post brought a letter from my younger brother, Arthur, at school at Taunton, saying that if I had to join the infantry, I should be sure to avoid joining the Somersets. His school had just been to the barracks and it was the nearest thing he could imagine to a concentration camp. A certain Sgt Lovell was obviously the devil incarnate!

With this intelligence to cheer me on, I set off for Taunton and the war. Sure enough, all the newly-arrived 'potential officers' were under the direct care of Sgt Lovell. He was certainly tough, but within a month he had won us completely. He made us believe we were the best platoon in the barracks and possibly in the British Army.

After some months, our platoon was sorted into those who were considered material to go on to an Officer Cadet Training Unit, and those who were found wanting. Twenty passed: seven, of whom I was one, failed.

We seven were all made temporary acting unpaid lance-corporals. But the Army did not know quite what to do with us. We discovered that when a unit does not know what to do with a man, they send him on a course. I went on several.

Then there was a whisper that volunteers were required for an Intelligence course. Unlike the other courses, this appealed tremendously to my ego. With another of the seven I was duly selected as a suitable candidate and off we went in high glee. We reported to the barracks of the Household Cavalry in Hyde Park.

Men of all ranks from private to captain were assembled there and we were taken to a room at the top of the building. Our instructor, a colonel in the Educational Corps, introduced himself. The door of the room was locked and we were asked to read and sign the Official Secrets Act. Next we were told we might take no notes, nor carry any paper out of the room. We had to learn and remember all we were taught. The course would consist of two hours in the morning and two in the afternoon. This was all the human brain could absorb of the subject we were to learn. By this time we were agog.

We were then brilliantly instructed by the colonel in the use of cipher. We soon gathered that to be good at cipher one needed a certain sort of brain. Some people are adept at crossword puzzles; others, like me, find them impossible. So it is with cipher. Past educational attainments meant little. You either had the knack or you hadn't.

I was delighted to find that I had. My companion, Cpl Durrant, from the Somersets, was the same. We finished at the top of the class and were marked men from that moment. We were suddenly 'important' to the War Office as trained high-grade cipher operators.

Durrant and I did not have to wait long before the War Office telephoned the Somersets and ordered them to despatch us immediately to GHQ British Expeditionary Force, France.

We were on the train that night. We got as far as Dover, when an order came through cancelling our boat. It was May 1940 and the Battle of France had reached the fluid stage with the breakthrough of the German panzers at Sedan. Durrant and I were back in Taunton the following night.

Within a week we set off again for Dover and this time had better luck. We boarded a troopship at dead of night, and sailed in the early hours across a sea on which we could see ships burning in the distance. Our companions were a battalion of the Welsh Guards. I watched the guardsmen writing postcards and letters to their friends and families.

For very many it was their last message. When we landed at Boulogne next morning they marched off the quay and dug in outside the town. That evening they took on German tanks with rifles and Bren guns and were over-run with very great losses.

We ourselves never got off the quay. We showed the transport officer our papers ordering us to GHQ. But there was chaos everywhere. Soldiers from many countries milled around looking for their units. No-one knew where the Germans were or where our army was.

Finally, we were advised to get on any boat returning to Britain, and then try and get another one to Dunkirk. With regret we joined the crowd of lost soldiery and scrambled aboard a ship. We later learned that we were about the last to get out of Boulogne before the Germans took the town.

But when we reached England confusion continued. We again showed our War Office orders directing us to GHQ. No-one would listen. On the contrary, we were given a hero's welcome, handed cups of tea and bars of chocolate by the Women's Volunteer Service and packed off to a staging camp on Salisbury Plain.

For a week we went from camp to camp trying to get transport to Dunkirk. One officer in despair sent us to the War Office in London. We walked into the Whitehall buildings with our kitbags. Even there, a harassed officer merely sent us to another staging camp. We gave up and decided to have a day at home before returning to the Somersets at Taunton.

I had my twenty-first birthday there, filling palliases with straw for soldiers still returning from France. In the evening I celebrated with Somerset cider, then cheap and potent: Later, the worse for wear, I went into a church to pray. I can't remember what about, but I did want to include God in a day that was important in my life. I was still a churchgoer, though occasional diversions, like casual ladies found in garrison towns, were entering in too.

I was then posted to Army HQ Aldershot. There I played cricket for Aldershot Command, batting with the man who had been my hero: Denis Compton. Alf Gover was also there; then, as ever, holding court and casting his spell, for few can tell a cricket story so well.

After some months at Aldershot I joined 4 Corps Headquarters, which was assigned to take charge of an Allied army in Iraq, put there to prevent the Germans capturing the Middle East oilfields.

We had been in Iraq only two weeks, however, when we were urgently ordered to Singapore to take command of the troops there. By the time we reached the Indian Ocean, Singapore had fallen, and we turned left into Bombay and settled down in the Fort at Ahmednagar. It was so hot in India I thought I would die. Then I discovered the miracle-working power of salt, and all was well.

Meanwhile the Japanese were sweeping across Burma and we were moved to the Burmese border to take charge of the remnants of the Allied armies retreating into India. We crossed India by road, an endless dusty line of trucks. It was during this journey that I decided to apply for a direct commission as a cipher officer.

When we reached Calcutta, we loaded our vehicles and equipment onto trains which took us to Dimapur, the railhead for Burma.

Now peacetime India was left behind, and we were in the atmosphere of war. Ragged soldiers and refugees were everywhere, and a baby was born on the station platform as we arrived.

After a day or two we began our trek up the winding mountain road to Manipur via Kohima. It was a spectacular road, with countless hairpin bends as it snaked its way round the precipitous, jungle-clad slopes. We counted more than fifty trucks that had plunged over the edge and down the mountainside.

We had heard that the Naga tribesmen of these parts were headhunters, and we observed with lively interest the long two-edged knives they carried up the length of their backs. The handles were level with their necks and the broad, curved bottom of the blade rested in a contrivance strapped around their waists. They were everywhere on the road.

High up in the mists of one mountain our convoy stopped and we were surrounded by a group of curious tribesmen. I got out my gramophone and started it up, hoping to distract their attention from any other activity they might have had in mind. Then one of them began to pass the time of day with me in the most cultured of Oxford accents. We all laughed.

We soon found that the Nagas were courageous allies. They did not like the Japanese and enthusiastically joined us in common cause.

We worked as I have never worked before. We were swamped by messages to cipher and decipher. Only cables with the highest priority stood a chance of being done in effective time. Others would sometimes wait a week.

I was furious at what I thought was the incompetent way the cipher organisation was run. I became impatient for news of my application for a commission and the chance this might give to try to remedy what appeared to me the weakest link in the army's communication system.

Eventually word came from GHQ in Delhi to say that the application of Sgt Dodds for a commission had been approved, and that he should report to Delhi forthwith. When my colonel heard of this, he shouted, 'If they want to commission Dodds, let him buy some pips and put them on here. I am not letting him go at this stage of the battle.' I was beside myself with frustration. I could not see the colonel's point of view, but I just had to stay.

What went on officially I do not know, but some months later, when the monsoon arrived, and operations let up a little, another message came through ordering me at once to Delhi. This time I went.

It was now 1942 and I was 23. Much had gone on in my spirit these last months and years which I would have found hard to express in words. I had no idea how to relate the faith I had been brought up in to the realities of everyday life. And now I wasn't so sure I wanted to learn.

I was about to be commissioned. For the first time I would have a social position, and more money to match. I began to desire what I considered a long overdue 'good time'. I wondered whether I could wangle the position of cipher officer in some romantic spot like Kabul, or Chungking, and there live it up.

These ideas were in my mind when I reached Delhi, plus a fierce conviction that the cipher organisation needed a complete overhaul, and I was the man to do it.

I walked into GHQ New Delhi, a sergeant from the Burma front, and confronted the staff captain in charge of cipher whose name was Ames. I intended giving him a piece of my mind and did so immediately. In the strongest terms I asked him what he thought he was up to. Did he know the conditions under which we operated, and the poor calibre of officers we had to do the job, and the hopeless organisation? We were shouting at each other in no time. There were two other officers in the room, and, with a glance at them, the staff captain recalled himself and said, 'Well, sergeant, why don't you take your hat off, pull up a chair and let's have a talk about all these matters.'

So we did. I told him how I would run things. We often laughed about it afterwards. But I felt strongly; and he let me get out all the steam.

Then he said, 'Dodds, I have started a cipher school here in Delhi. The next course begins in a couple of weeks and I would like you to take it before you are commissioned.' I told Capt. Ames I did not want to go on any cipher course as I knew it all backwards. His eyes twinkled. 'Well,' he said, 'I think you should — just as a matter of routine.'

He then asked me if I would like to have a holiday before the course began or would I prefer to use the time working in the cipher office in GHQ getting further experience.

Ambition led me to choose the latter. So Capt. Ames took me down to the cipher office and introduced me to the man in charge, Major Ronald Cohen. Ames introduced me as 'Sgt Dodds, who would like to work for you for two weeks and show you how to run your office!'

Major Cohen watched for his opportunity, and did not have long to wait. In GHQ I was confronted with types of cipher I had not met before. Pride prevented me from asking for too much help and I soon made a bad mistake. In front of everybody, Major Cohen gave me an outsize telling off.

Delhi was a turning point for me in another way. One Sunday evening I attended Evensong. As I left the church I took the decision that had long been maturing in my mind — never to go to church again until I knew why I went, and how I could relate religion to everyday life. At least this was what I told myself. But my motives were mixed. I was also swayed by the thought of the opportunities which my promotion opened up for the 'good life'. Religion might place restraints.

The cipher course went well but not as well as I hoped. I got a B-plus instead of an A. My downfall came over fishplates. In our final test we had to decipher a message which consisted of a long order for army stores and equipment. One item, according to my deciphering, was for several hundred fishplates. As this seemed to me to be a ridiculous luxury even for the leisurely pace at which the war in India was then proceeding, I feverishly set about trying to unravel what I felt must be a mistake and came up with some ingenious alternative. But fishplates it was. I often remember this now whenever I travel by train and see the things in their thousands binding rails to sleepers.

Within days I was commissioned. I went out and bought a new uniform, but was not posted to the glamorous spot I half-hoped for. I was sent to start a new cipher section in 33 Indian Corps, then being formed in South India.

As I waited on the station for the train, I was approached by a small boy selling very second-hand books. I looked through his titles and found one called *Innocent Men* by Peter Howard. I bought it, thinking it might be a sequel to the political book, *Guilty Men*, which I had earlier enjoyed so much. I soon discovered it to be not about politics but about a political journalist who investigated Moral Re-Armament with the idea of exposing it but ended up espousing it. It was in the same pungent style as *Guilty Men*, which was not surprising since, as I learned later, Peter Howard had been co-author of the earlier book.

As we rumbled south through the subcontinent, I told my travelling companion, a lieutenant-colonel returning from a course in jungle warfare, about the exciting book I was reading. He warned me to be very careful of Moral Re-Armament.

Our Headquarters were in a camp at Vanyanbadi, in scrub country halfway between Bangalore and Madras. I plunged at once into the challenge of my job and into the social opportunities of my new rank.

But after a few weeks I got a bad sore throat. I was ambitiously climbing and would not have dreamt of taking time off, but I did mention this sore throat to our medical officer, an Aberdonian. He peered into my open mouth.

'Good heavens!' he exclaimed, 'you've certainly a nasty throat. You must get to bed at once.' I told him such a thing was impossible: I had important work. I went on, 'I'm amazed the medical profession hasn't devised a better method of curing sore throats than sending people to bed.' 'Your trouble's self-importance,' said the doctor. And he went his way and I mine.

There days later I was in hospital with tonsilitis. The Aberdeen doctor came to see me. He brought with him certain reading material, some about Moral Re-Armament. But by this time I had put Moral Re-Armament on the shelf.

Junior officers were housed four to a bamboo 'basha' in this camp. One of those in my basha became by aider and abettor on the social opportunities road. Larger and larger quantities of drink were consumed, and when our first leave came up, we set off for Bombay with the intention of painting the town red.

On arrival we made straight for the Harbour Bar of the Taj Mahal Hotel. When we had ordered our drinks, an attractive girl came over to speak to an officer who had joined us. I got to know her well in the next days. It seemed I was not to escape Moral Re-Armament: all her family were in it, she told me. 'I think their ideas are good,' she said, 'but I mean to have a good time before I try them.'

That made two of us. Most nights, as soon as I was drunk I took a taxi for the red-light district.

Back in Vanyanbadi, I built a cricket pitch, hiring labour out of my own pay to clear boulders from the ground. We raised a team and had several matches against local Indian sides, mainly men who worked on the railways.

Our Headquarters were moved to Poona. On my way I spent two days in Bangalore. A blonde girl in my hotel caught my attention. I introduced myself and was at once captivated by her. That evening I asked her to marry me. The proposal was neither accepted nor rejected.

Next day we went our separate ways: she to join her brigadier father who was serving in the north, and I to Poona, in a high state of emotion. I wrote home to say I had found the girl I wanted to marry and I sent long daily letters to the lady. For a short while I became a reformed character.

In Poona, I began to play cricket for the Poona Club. I did so well as a bowler that I got an invitation to play for the Europeans in what was then the leading Indian cricket tournament. It took place in Bombay between five teams: the Hindus, the Muslims, the Parsees, the Europeans, and the Rest.

My self-confidence as a bowler was so great by this time that I felt I could bowl anybody out. I sent a telegram to my Bangalore girlfriend asking her to come and decorate the match.

Then the blow fell. Just before I was due to leave for Bombay and glory, my former trouble struck me down and I got severe tonsilitis. The Aberdonian doctor, David Watson, was summoned, but despite this I was very ill and could not play.

The match took place. The lady, not knowing of my sickness because of communication problems, came and found I was inexplicably missing. Her next letter told of plans to marry someone else: plans promptly carried out.

I therefore plunged once more into the social round. Things got to the point where I was generally in an unsteady state by dinner time. Every Saturday night most of the officers of our mess would go out on the town and return hilariously and noisily in the early hours. One could gain popularity by being in the forefront of this.

I seemed to have found the secret of how to get on in life. I felt extremely happy. And not only was I accepted by the fast set in the mess, but my cricket continued to prosper. I was chosen to play in another major match in Bombay. It was for the Services against an Indian eleven, a four-day game to raise funds for the Indian Red Cross.

The game was played in the Brabourne Stadium, which has been described as the most beautiful and symmetrical in the world. Its stands hold fifty thousand and the pavilion has every facility, including living accommodation for the teams, and a swimming pool.

In the Services eleven were several first-class cricketers like Joe Hardstaff and Harold Butler, who both played for England, and the captain was one of cricket's greatest characters, D. R. Jardine. To me he was an almost legendary figure, since he had captained England when I was a schoolboy, and won a famous, if controversial, victory over Australia.

My impression of Jardine was of a man with whom you had to have either a good or a bad relationship. He was not neutral. He sort of came at you, and began to probe your character. After our final practice session he sat beside me in the dressing-room. I was impressed by the nonchalant way he peeled off the vast amount of plaster that appeared to be holding together his ageing muscles. Then he said, 'Well Dodds, what are you going to bowl tomorrow and how do you plan to get these men out?' I had very little idea, which was probably what he wanted to find out.

Before the game started Jardine called us all together. 'Gentlemen,' he said, 'we have got to make this game last four days.' Then he gave us the shortest and soundest batting advice I have ever heard. 'Don't forget, batting is simple. All you have to do is put the bat to the ball.'

And this is what he did. Everyone had bowled Jardine out in the practice nets. But when it came to the game he applied his own advice and stayed in all one afternoon — putting bat to ball.

When India went in, our seam bowlers made little impression on what I have since discovered is one of the easiest batting wickets in the world. I was called up from the boundary as first change bowler. I really thought I was going to bowl India out. There was a gentleman called Mushtaq Ali batting. He proceeded to hit me all over Bombay. I had never experienced anything like it.

After one onslaught, I asked Jardine if I could move a man to that part of the field to which the last two boundaries had been despatched. 'No,' he said. I bowled another ball and Mushtaq sent it to the same place.

Next over someone was out, and I saw Jardine coming towards me. I was on the boundary and the crowd picked up his authoritarian figure heading in my direction. They chanted, 'left, right, left, right,' as he came. 'Dodds,' he barked, when within earshot, 'now listen to me. You and I are amateurs. It is only professionals who ask to have their field shifted when they are hit for four.' Then he turned round and marched back again. I was dumbstruck. Douglas Jardine was a man you did not forget.

I got one wicket — that of Rusi Modi, allegedly lbw. And in our second innings I managed to stay in most of one afternoon scoring 14, while Joe Hardstaff hit a century.

At this point, in late November 1944, far away on the frontier with Burma, the Japanese were again on the attack.

CHAPTER 4

Road to Mandalay

It was now the turn of 33 Corps Headquarters to be summoned to the Burma front. Once more I crossed India by road and rail and found myself at Dimapur.

This time the Japanese were only a few miles away. I spent the first night in a dugout in the jungle as the officer on duty. When I climbed down into this six-foot-square hole I saw, in the light of my hurricane lamp, that I was not alone. My companion was the biggest lizard I had ever seen, perhaps two feet long. From the look in his eye and the sharpness of his teeth it was evident that no amicable compromise was going to be reached. He put up a sharp fight before he was despatched.

The Japanese were astride the road just outside Dimapur. They had laid seige to Kohima, a town of great tactical importance since it lies at the summit of a pass 4700 ft high between the precipitous 10,000 ft massif to the west and the less impressive but still formidable ranges to the north-west. This pass is the only practical route for a highway between India and central Burma.

The beleaguered Kohima garrison, supplied by air, were holding out with great heroism. But their relief was urgent. This was the task of the Allied troops now arriving and under the command of our Headquarters.

For the next days a tough battle was fought mile by mile along this Dimapur-Kohima Road. The Second British Division, many of whom had spent much of the war up to this point in training, went into action with tremendous spirit. Their casualties were high but the Japanese began to go backwards and never really stopped doing so after that time.

The spirit among the Allied troops was very different from the defeatism prevalent when I was on this front before. Now everything seemed possible. There was nothing one would not do or tackle.

One reason for this change of spirit was that our forces had come to terms with jungle fighting. British troops have always been good at improvising, and now they had learned to improvise in jungle warfare. General Wingate's commando-style Chindit campaigns of the previous two years had proved to the British troops that they could survive the toughest conditions and beat the enemy.

We had become a 'can do' army, and we now had a 'can do' Supreme Commander: Admiral Lord Louis Mountbatten. When he took charge of our theatre of the war we quickly felt the inspiration of his fresh spirit.

Under Mountbatten was another down-to-earth fighting general, 'Bill' Slim; and we in 33 Corps thought a lot of our own man, General Monty Stopford. We were called the Forgotten Army, but the will to win was present and was decisive. The Japanese continued slowly retreating.

I was responsible for equipping all the units under our command with a continuous stream of fresh ciphers, and for making sure that they were never compromised through loss or other means and that the ciphers that had been used were properly destroyed. After the cipher chaos during my earlier spell on this front, I was determined that nothing like it would happen under my responsibility. Like the rest of our army at that time I was bursting with confidence that we could do all that was asked of us.

One Saturday night in my mess, in our camp on Bulldozer Ridge overlooking the plains of Burma, we invited as guests members of the WASB — Women's Auxiliary Service Burma.

I sat next to a girl whose name and picture had frequently been in the glossy social magazines of India. It had surprised me to read of her leaving the social whirl of India for the Burma front. I studied her with interest. She was very attractive and lively.

After dinner, having discovered her interest in music, I fetched my gramophone and serenaded her with the aid of Beethoven and Chopin, the Ink Spots and Glenn Miller.

Next day one of the other officers and I received an invitation to lunch in the mess of the WASB. We spruced up and went. I was puzzled to know why I had been singled out for preferment when there were many thousands of men in the army in Burma and attractive ladies were so limited in number.

Lunch merged into tea, and tea to dinner. The gramophone again floated out its melodies as we sat outside the mess tent in the cool mountain air, the fireflies flickering, the night-time noises of the jungle in the background, and a three-quarter moon softly lighting up the dark tropical sky.

Paulette, for that is the name I will give her, was, I discovered, going on leave the next day. She was also due to be moved from that particular WASB unit at the end of her leave. So I did not expect to see her again.

We now moved out of the mountainous region, crossed the Chindwin River on the longest Bailey bridge ever constructed, and were in the plains of Burma. The advance on Mandalay had begun.

A week or two later I received a long letter from Paulette from India, plus a recording of Beethoven's Violin Concerto which she commended with her love. And unbeknown to me she was using her considerable charm and influence to get her new posting cancelled and herself returned to her old unit.

One day my brigadier, who knew of the development with Paulette, called me into his tent and informed me she had arrived back in camp. He told me to take his jeep and go and meet the girl. He was always proud of the achievements of his staff.

I saluted and retired. The trouble was I couldn't drive a jeep. I decided to try and bluff it out and climbed into the vehicle. I explained the extreme jerkiness of our drive to a puzzled Paulette by pointing to the roughness of the track.

Somehow we made it to her tent, unloaded her gear and went inside. While we were within, darkness fell. I was unaware that in fiddling with the switches of the jeep I had turned on the headlights. Soon there was an almighty commotion. The guard came rushing round with the Brigadier General Staff to know what the hell was going on and who was breaking the blackout. But when the brigadier (not my brigadier) discovered who were the occupants of the tent, I was surprised how indulgent he became.

In the next six months Paulette and I saw each other almost daily.

The Allied forces advancing south were now within striking distance of Mandalay. The Japanese were well dug in and were expecting a major frontal assault on the city and along the banks of the mighty Irrawaddy to the west.

The Allies then decided on a plan in which wireless and cipher deception played a vital role.

The idea was for a considerable part of the Allied army facing the

Japanese to withdraw under wireless silence and the greatest secrecy. They would then march south making a wide detour round and behind the Japanese positions.

Meanwhile duplicate signals and cipher units would be left behind and would continue to send out and receive messages, which would now be dummy ones, aimed at deceiving the Japanese that the army was in its original position. One stupid signal or cipher error could have given the game away.

All went according to plan and our phantom army suddenly burst on the main supply and administrative base of the Japanese army south of Mandalay, at Meiktila. Great havoc was wrought among these rear echelons. The Japanese army was now cut off and like a nut in a nutcracker. Although they fought with their usual courage and tenacity there was great slaughter and their units became increasingly scattered in the jungle on either side of the central Burmese plain.

Before long we were racing for Rangoon. Paulette asked me to take her in my jeep, which I now could drive. I was dubious, imagining becoming the butt of much ribaldry from the troops we passed. But the four-day dash to the capital went well.

Soon the war in Europe was ended, and so was the mopping-up of the scattered and defeated Japanese army in Burma. Our own forces were reorganised: 33 Corps Headquarters became 12 Army Headquarters, centred on the university.

It was a return to static soldiering. I began to think of the future.

CHAPTER 5

Back to Cricket with a Difference

My old Barclays Bank cricket captain, Nobby Hunt, wrote to me at this time saying that if I wanted to play county cricket after the war, he thought Essex was the club to try. He explained that he had played with some of the team in wartime matches and found them 'a fine lot'.

To play county cricket was certainly my ambition. I even took the precaution of fiddling my release group from the army one group earlier than it should have been so that I would be free to play at the start of the post-war season.

But like many others in the army I was also thinking in a larger perspective and wondering how a better world could be constructed after the war was over.

There were in our mess in Rangoon two men who talked of this in global terms. One was a communist. He was an architect, who later became a leading town-planner. He said the capitalist system was the main problem and had to go. Human intelligence was the thing: you had to have centrallised control and planning. The end would justify the means. If people objected they would in the final analysis be dealt with by force. 'We've killed millions of people in war to no good purpose. What's wrong with killing people in peace for a good purpose?' he said on one occasion; and to me, at that time, this did not seem very unreasonable.

The other man who talked in world terms of a better society was David Watson, now a colonel at our headquarters. He said the changes needed in the world would happen as men decided to accept absolute moral standards as the guide to the conduct of their lives an public affairs: by men who said they wanted to put right the wrong things in the world and started by first putting right the places where they themselves were wrong. Above all by men who abandoned their own self-willed plans and accepted God's plan fc. their lives instead. Watson maintained that this could answer the cause of conflict between men and nations who now, when the chips were down, fought to get their own way.

I decided to watch the architect and the doctor and see how their ideas worked out in their own lives. I made a very interesting discovery.

I found the architect, despite his well-articulated ideas and dedication, to be full of bitterness, fear, and a consuming personal ambition. I said to myself that an idea and philosophy that did not deal with these things in people would not do what is necessary in the world, for these were just the sort of problems that caused the trouble.

When I came to look closely at the doctor's life I found he had a freedom in such matters. I became convinced that his ideas were the right ones because they dealt with the root of the trouble: the wrong things in people which led to all the other wrongs.

By this time Paulette was becoming alarmed at the new ideas I was considering. The Japanese had now capitulated. I had been four years overseas and was due to return to England. Paulette decided to continue with the army across Asia to Japan.

Her last gift to me before I boarded my ship for England was a book of bawdy stories, with a note to say she hoped I had not lost my ability to enjoy such things.

This book led to a remarkable experience I had on the boat. I spent most of the time in the ship's hospital with jaundice. I lent the book to one of the nursing sisters. In return she lent me a book of essays, one of which was about mankind's seemingly universal need of a God.

I fell to thinking of Watson's ideas and of my difficulty in accepting them because I had cut myself off from God. Suddenly it flooded in on me that the God I had come to know in my youth through Jesus was loving and forgiving. I felt God loved and forgave me. The way to Him was open. It was so deep an emotional experience that the ward seemed to glow with an amber warmth.

I expected life to be different after this, but was surprised to find that nothing altered.

When I got home I returned immediately to my father's vicarage at Hatton in Warwickshire. One of the first things I did was to get in touch with Nobby Hunt, who introduced me to the captain of the Essex County Cricket Club, T. N. Pearce.

Also living at my father's vicarage were my younger brother, Arthur, and his wife Letty. Arthur had been in the RAF. His plane had been shot down over the North African desert. During a seven-day march trying to reach his own lines, he had made the decision to let God run his life.

He was captured but, with companions, escaped from his prisoner of war camp in Italy. The escape was a thrilling one. At a crucial point Arthur turned to God for direction and had a clear but dangerous thought. With some trepidation he proposed it to his companions. They accepted it and it enabled the whole party to reach freedom.

He had since married an officer in the Women's Auxiliary Air Force. Both, I was surprised to find, were committed to the same ideas as David Watson. So there were two people on the spot with whom I could continue my discussions. As an aid to these deliberations I ordered a barrel of beer and installed it in my father's study.

I immediately noticed my brother had an inner authority which I could not influence. In our relationship before I had been able to wield considerable power over him, perhaps because I was older. Now he always seemed to turn to this authority for direction. There was a rock on which he stood, while my feet were on shifting sand. I envied this rock. When I asked him how I could find it too, he pointed me to the same course of action which David had done: I must ask God what to do, and do it.

I wanted to help build a new world. But was I prepared to pay the price by letting God control such money as I had, whom I married, what job I did and how I did it, how I spent all my time?

'Why,' I said to my brother, 'it's like dying!'

He said it was but that there was a new life to follow.

'How can one be sure?'

'You can't,' he said, 'it's only a promise. But you have the assurance that God loves you and only wants the best for you.'

'Can I have a prospectus of what He has in store, so I can weigh up whether it's worth it?'

'If you could, it would not be the step in faith you need to take.'

The time for decision was at hand. Sitting in a deckchair on the vicarage lawn on a warm spring morning in 1946 I decided that so far as I could understand it I would from that point only do what

God told me to do. The decision took a moment of time. With it I stepped into a new world.

The first thing I did after making this decision was to put my hand down for a cigarette. Then I thought, 'God has not told you to have a cigarette,' so I pulled my hand up again.

Next I made a list under the heading of Honesty of the things I could see I needed to put right. There was army equipment which had found its way into my possession: I bundled it up and returned it as soon as I could. Then there was my fiddled release group. I hesitated. Was it really wise to put this right? Suppose the Army accepted my right time for release? Would that not jeopardise my chances of getting into a county team and establishing a place? But I realised this must be an all-or-nothing experiment. So I decided to tell the Army what I had done. A few days later I heard from the Army, to my dismay, that they had put back my release group. I also wrote to Paulette telling her of the decision I had made. It was the final break. She later married a general.

Back with my unit in Yorkshire for my final stint with the Army, each morning when I woke I began to practise the two-way telephone conversation of prayer and then of being quiet to see what thoughts God might want to give me in return.

How do I know that the thoughts I get are God's thoughts and not my own? My answer is that there can be no absolute certainty, and that the thoughts that do come need to be checked against the absolute standards which Christ spoke about and demonstrated in His life — absolute honesty, purity, unselfishness, and love. Another test is to check one's thoughts with others who are also committed to doing God's will. In the end one has to go ahead in faith. As each step is taken in faith it is possible to look back, like a man on the stern of a ship looking back at its wake, and see how God has steered one past this or that obstacle, and how this or that thought, obeyed, has borne fruit. So is faith strengthened. That is the way charted in the Bible, and one should not, I suppose, be amazed that it works.

One of the things I needed clarity on was what to do when I finally left the Army in a few weeks' time. As a result of meeting Tom Pearce, I now received an invitation to come for a trial at the Essex nets at Chelmsford. Since these arrangements with Essex had been made before by decision to let God run my life, I did not know whether it was right to go ahead with them.

Nothing came clear. Then I had the thought to apply for leave to go; if God did not wish it, some stop would come somewhere along the line. None did. Leave was immediately granted and I took a train to Chelmsford.

I had never seen Essex before, and as I looked at the rows of East End houses and then the flat lands beyond I did not like what I saw.

I booked into a hotel and went down to the ground for my 'trial'. As I joined the other players in the nets Ray Smith came up to greet me. He introduced me to the other players, who gave me a welcome that made me feel immediately included in what was going on.

I had gone to Essex mainly as a leg-break bowler. Several players in the Essex nets seemed to bowl leg-breaks better than I did. There was Peter Smith, who later played for England, and Frank Vigar and Reg Taylor, who bowled them left-handed.

Jack O'Connor, the old Essex and England batsman, was in charge of the trial that day. At the end of the morning, after I had batted, he came up to me and said he thought I was just the man they were looking for to open the Essex innings. I was amazed.

I returned to the Army. Because I had got straight on the question of my release date I was still there when the cricket season began. Someone else was opening the innings for Essex and was doing it very well. I felt rather bitter towards God. I had tried to do the right thing and as a result it looked as though I was going to lose my chance. Then I did something I had not tried before in such situations. I prayed about it. A great peace came into me and a compelling certainty that all would be well.

CHAPTER 6

'Hit the Ball Hard and Enjoy It'

I was demobbed on May 20, and on the 21st I took my mother on an expedition to London. On our return there was a telegram from Essex waiting, asking me to play the following day against Sussex at Ilford.

There was scarcely time to think. I packed my cricket gear and caught the first train to London the next morning. I did not know where Ilford was. At Paddington a porter opened the carriage door and got my bags and asked where I wanted to go. I said, 'Ilford, quick.'

He then led me up the back end of Paddington station. I did not know there was a tube station there, and, as we went, I almost thought my cause was lost. However, the porter knew his job and I caught an underground at once for Liverpool Street, where I got an immediate connection for Ilford. Outside Ilford station there was a solitary taxicab — in the days when cabs were almost non-existent.

I got to the ground with just enough time to change and join the Essex side as they took the field. I reflected, as we walked out, that by that very act I had got my name in *Wisden*!

Our turn came to bat in the evening. Jim Cornford opened the bowling for Sussex. When I had scored 18, he had me caught at the wicket by Billy Griffith. I was rather disappointed.

I stayed that night in a hotel in Chelmsford. Next morning I woke early and took time to pray and ask God about the day. My prayer went something like this: 'OK, God, I'll open the innings for Essex, but how do you want me to play?'

Immediately there came into my mind the thought, 'Hit the ball hard and enjoy it.'

I could not pretend the thought had not come. It had. I had asked the question. Back came the answer. I protested. It was dangerous.

Opening bats did not play in this fashion. Why, you might get out. No, no, no! God did not seem inclined to argue.

I decided not to obey. It was absolutely contrary to the way I played. I was full of caution, and cricket was a most serious business.

In the second innings I got 63, very slowly. We drew the match and I should think that while I batted some of the spectators went to sleep.

One thing that struck me at once was the fellowship of first-class cricketers. It was a fellowship into which one was immediately included by playing county cricket and by no other means. Until you played you were out: once you had played you were in. You were called by your first name by all in this fellowship from that point on.

After the match we changed and took a train to Portsmouth for the game next day against Hampshire. My cricket career was launched. As we walked out of the pavilion that evening and across the ground a swarm of small boys asked for the players' autographs. Tom Pearce, seeing my diffidence, said, 'Go on Dickie, you might as well start now. It's something you've got to get used to.'

I did not get many runs in my first few matches, and I was beginning to feel very insecure about my place in the side. I had no idea how teams were selected, so I thought I would make the first move and I asked Tom Pearce, as we were leaving after one game, whether he required me for the next. I had the feeling the Skipper, as he and all county captains are called by the players, knew exactly what was going on in my heart. It was one of his gifts as captain. He laughed and, in a way that won my allegiance from then on, said I was definitely needed.

I had come to Essex purely as a cricketer, and had been accepted by my team-mates as such. I began to feel guilty because I knew these new friends of mine, whose company I enjoyed, did not know the real man they were accepting. I did not want any longer to act a double role. How to tell them the basis I had accepted for my life?

I did not have long to wait. One Sunday as we sat in the Ship Hotel in Brighton, relaxing and talking, Tom Wade our wicket-keeper, began to probe me with questions and it all came out.

Tom is one of the straightest men I have met. He is also one of the strongest. His brother was a professional wrestler, and Tom too had made his appearances in the ring. The only time I ever saw

Tom angry was when someone in our side suggested that the grunt-and-groan profession was not as honest as it might be. The glint in Tom's eye, and the bulge of his muscles, ensured that this was not a subject made light of again.

I was glad Tom drew out my convictions. I was now exposed, but my team-mates knew where I stood. I had to work out my new life with them as well as with cricket itself, though as far as this went, I had firmly put aside the thought of hitting the ball hard and enjoying it.

One day I arrived to play against Surrey at The Oval, short of runs and low in spirits. Surrey batted first and were all out by mid-afternoon. As I stood at the top of the steps in the pavilion with my opening partner, 'Sonny' Avery, I asked him if he would take first ball. I thought if he did this, I would at least be in no danger of returning at once to the pavilion. Such was the state of my confidence, but in fact we were still there at close of play with Essex 235 for none.

One of the Surrey bowlers that sunny afternoon was Alf Gover, in the autumn of his long career. In frustration he came up to me and said what a beautiful batting wicket it was, with the strong innuendo that it was brutal punishment to have to bowl on such a pitch. In my innocence, the only reply I could think of was to remark that all the Surrey batsmen had managed to get out on this beautiful wicket only an hour or so before, for 162. I was told that Alf added this to his inexhaustible fund of anecdotes.

On Monday morning, 'Sonny' and I took the score to 270, a new Essex first-wicket record, before I was out for 103. When I returned to our dressing-room, Tom Pearce awarded me my county cap. This meant I was now a fully-fledged county cricketer.

Players and enthusiasts all agree that cricket is a funny game. By this they do not mean that it makes for side-splitting laughter — though it sometimes does — but that you can never be certain what will happen next. This is part of the fascination of the game. One minute you don't know where your next run will come from and the next you have broken a record. I was delighted and went straight off to Foster's in Bruton Street to order myself an Essex blazer.

But things were not right. There was that unobeyed thought about hitting the ball hard. Some weeks later we were playing Warwickshire at Birmingham. I stayed at home for this game against the county for which I had once hoped to play. I made seven in the first innings, and six in the second. My father and mother had never entertained a gloomier son. How do you help a man in this situation?

My brother Arthur, who was at home at the time, did the trick. He was now studying theology at Oxford and had become a sensitive soul surgeon. He probed prayerfully the mind of God as to what he should do, and he did a very funny thing. Just as I left the house for our next match against Middlesex at Westcliff-on-Sea, he handed me a note to read on the train. It ran: 'There was once a small boy who was playing football. He ran down the left wing and cut in, and scored a beautiful goal. His face lit up, and he looked up, and said, ''Look, Jesus, what I've done!'''

I got the idea. 'Hit the ball hard and enjoy it.' Of course, this was it. A God who loved beautiful things would not love the dull old cricket I played. Nor, in my deepest heart, did I. The thing I most enjoyed was the creation of beautiful strokes. The decision was made. From now on, the thought that had come during that first county match was going to be obeyed.

I got top score, 61 and 72, in each innings of our match against Middlesex, and, while batting, I felt closer to God than ever before in my life. I tried to fashion the loveliest strokes I could manage for the God who would enjoy them. In return, I had a tremendous sense of His pleasure.

At the end of the game the captain of Middlesex and former England captain, R. W. V. Robins, came into our dressing-room, stuck out his hand, and said, 'Dickie, I want to congratulate you on the way you play cricket.'

In the next game, against Hampshire, I got to 98 on the basis of hitting the ball hard and enjoying it. I then thought to myself, 'Go steady for your century.'

It was as though the sun had gone in, or a tap had been turned off. I could not understand what had happened. There was a barrenness. Then I remembered — I had said 'No' to God, and taken up my old material safety-first philosophy. I threw it all out, hit the next ball over mid-off for four, and that was that.

There was another significant incident in that match. During my innings I hooked at a ball and got a very faint touch. The only man who suspected I had hit it was short leg. He made a half-hearted appeal which was turned down. Afterwards I told some of our players that I had hit the ball. This word got to the umpire, who took it up with me very strongly. He said that I should never discuss umpire's decisions or I would get a bad reputation with them, and it would be the worse for me.

I was puzzled to know why I had had no sense of God's displeasure at staying in when I was out, but a very strong sense of His displeasure when I began playing safe at 98. Perhaps the answer lies in motive. It had not been in my mind to cheat. I longed to stay in to bat in this new way and looked on it as good fortune that I had not been given out.

However, I later decided that, since the Laws said that if you hit the ball and were caught, you were out — then those were the rules. You rarely needed an umpire to tell you whether you had hit the ball. From that time on, if I knew I had hit the ball, and someone had caught it, out I walked.

This got me into trouble once or twice. One day I was playing against Fred Trueman on a dodgy wicket, with the ball flying all over the place. I played at a ball, there was a loud snick, and Fred and all Yorkshire appealed with a roar to the heavens. But, though I would have been more than glad in one way to have retired at that point, I could not honestly claim to have touched the ball. So I stayed where I was and the umpire turned down the appeal. What Johnny Wardle, the Yorkshire spin bowler, said to me at the end of the over is unprintable.

Another time I hit the ball hard, and the wicketkeeper caught it and appealed loudly. I had turned and gone by the wicketkeeper on my way to the pavilion when the umpire said 'Not out'. I did not know what to do. I tried to look as though I was taking a stroll round the wicketkeeper to calm my nerves. Then I resumed my innings in a rather more carefree manner till I was out.

Another issue of conscience soon arose. One Sunday, a charity match was arranged between Essex and an England eleven to raise money for a hospital. Did God want me to play cricket on a Sunday?

I got on my knees and wrestled with this problem, on which my mind was open. There was God's command about not working on a Sunday. Was this work? Did one, by playing, make others work — train-drivers, bus-drivers, gatemen, groundsmen? Yet the cause was good. Nothing came very clear. Then somewhat to my surprise, I felt I should play in this match.

The other side batted first on a fine day, with some 3000 people watching, including a great number of children. When Essex batted

I was soon out, so I got changed. After tea I left the ground and strolled up the road. I came across a church in which the evening service was about to begin, and I went inside.

There was a handful of people in the congregation and three small boys in the choir. I compared these three boys with the hundreds just down the road watching their heroes play cricket. What sort of example was being set? That was the end of Sunday cricket for me. I was somewhat apprehensive about my colleagues' reactions, but Tom Pearce merely said, 'Well, Jack Hobbs never did either.'

That first summer advanced with our team moving from one tented field in Essex to another. By now I was growing to love the county, with its strong and invigorating air, its marshes, and gently undulating countryside, the cornfields, sea and estuary, and those beautiful villages which seemed to contain picturesque old cottages in larger numbers than anywhere else in England.

As the season moved towards its end I realised that another decision was going to have to be made. What did God want me to do with my life by way of an occupation? Did He want me to go on playing cricket, or did He want me to go back to Barclays Bank, where my job was still open? Or was there something else? I decided that when the time came, God would show me. I prayed about it and left it in His hands.

But when our last game arrived I was no clearer. The match was against Gloucester, at the Waggon Works ground in that town. We stayed at the New Inn — which had been new in the 15th century and hadn't changed much in outward appearance since. It was a delightful spot.

With no clarity in my mind as to what I should do at the end of those three days in Gloucester, I prayed harder than ever. I even tried the Cathedral to see if I could get my query through, and, more important, a reply. Nothing came. So, when everyone else went home at the end of the match, I decided to check in again at the New Inn, and stay there until I knew what was the right move.

That night I sat down to think it all through once more. Suddenly fresh light came. I realised I had been asking God to agree to my continuing to play cricket. I did not want to go back to banking. I had not been free in my spirit and willing to do whatever God said. My prayer had not been so much a prayer as a demand.

Seeing this brought great freedom. I still did not want to return to banking, but was now willing. In fact, I went to bed that night believing this was what I was to do. Next morning when I awoke I began to wonder which branch of the bank I would be sent to.

Then, as I shaved, I remembered with great vividness the story of Abraham and Isaac. Abraham greatly loved his son. One day God told him to take Isaac up the mountain and offer him as a sacrifice. This deeply grieved Abraham, but because he had decided to obey the voice of God in his heart, he resolved to do it. Father and son set off up the mountain. Then, when the deed was about to be done, God told Abraham to stop. He now knew that Abraham really loved Him more than his son and was ready to obey Him in everything.

I knew at that moment that cricket was what God wanted me to do. He had had to get me to the place where I was willing to give it up before He could with certainty show me what was right.

There was a very great joy in my heart as I returned home that day.

The next point to decide was whether to be amateur or professional. I felt that if you were going to give your whole time to playing cricket and had no private resources on which to live then you should be paid for it openly. I knew there were various ways in which one could be paid and yet retain amateur status. Somehow this did not seem to be in line with the spirit of the revolution to which I had committed myself. So I signed a professional agreement with Essex and sent it off to Mr Castor, the county secretary.

The agreement was for a year and ran from October to October. I was to receive £450, paid in monthly instalments, for the cricket services I rendered to the county, plus such talent and win money as might be awarded. The latter, together with fees from festival matches played at the end of the season and from an MCC match or two, might add another £100.

I thought much about this amateur/professional problem. It never worried me during my career because of the basis on which my own decision had been made. But it sometimes aroused strong feelings in others.

Having played my first season as an amateur I experienced both sides of the fence. On my first visit to the Old Trafford ground, for instance, I lunched upstairs in the pavilion with the other amateurs and Lancashire officials. And very fine it was, with brandy and cigars to finish with for those who wished. The next time I visited Old Trafford I trooped to a dining-room below the dressing-rooms with the other pros and the fare was much plainer.

I also remember there was a time when Essex played away matches during which, while we all stayed at the same hotel, paid for by the county, the professionals had to have a meal within a price limit or pay the extra themselves, while the amateurs could have their fling. This caused some momentary feeling but it never amounted to much. The camaraderie and general enjoyment of life and cricket among the Essex players was too great for much of that. Some counties went to far greater lengths. I remember being surprised to see one professional doff his hat to his county captain and say 'Good morning, sir' in a deferential tone. Then, and to this day, that county has had trouble between its officials and players.

My own view of the amateur and professional problem was that the real solution was to have only players. Those who wished would be paid; and those who did not so wish, and were able to support themselves, could do that. This, in time, was the way things worked out.

CHAPTER 7

County Round: April-May

While much has been written on Test cricket, many people have asked me what the life of an ordinary county cricketer was like. We will live through an imaginary season.

County cricket before the advent of the 'one-day game' was a comparatively uncomplicated affair. The season started early in May and went straight through to the end of August, with one three-day match following another. Occasionally there was a gap with no fixture, but the impression was of four months' continuous cricket. It was a wonderful way of life for those who had the good fortune to play then.

I can still almost taste the atmosphere and feeling and smell of those early April days when the Essex players reported for their first nets of the new season. After the constraints of indoor winter jobs, and long dark winter evenings, it was a joy, and gave a marvellous feeling of freedom to be in flannels and run on the newly-mown turf. And there was the inviting sight of the freshly rolled and cut net wickets — the green of the turf set off by the glistening white of the bowling and batting creases.

In those days we would begin straight away with net practice. The opening batsmen would be asked to pad up, and a little self-consciously we would go to the crease (for we had spent the winter in anonymous activity and had got out of the habit of being looked at) and take guard. The bowlers were no less self-conscious, wondering where their first delivery would pitch, if at all. And so, creakily, it would all begin — another summer of history to be recorded in *Wisden*.

Those first seasons after the war seem very carefree in retrospect. I am sure we were not as fit as we should have been. In Essex, at any rate, physiotherapists, trainers and managers were unknown.

But it was not long before the county moved with the times, and instead of nets we began the season with weight-training and had a full-time physiotherapist to repair the damage to muscles unaccustomed to such violence.

Perhaps I should have done better had I been fitter. I made a serious attempt to achieve this once. I had spent the winter in Stoke-on-Trent. The Port Vale football ground was not far from where I lived and as the season grew nearer I decided I would burst on the cricket scene as the fastest man in the county. Port Vale were glad to let me train on their ground and every afternoon I used to run round their pitch.

The only result of all this activity was that I damaged both achilles tendons and played the whole of the next season with them strapped up and in much discomfort. I was never much of an enthusiast for pre-season training after that.

After a week of nets or sometimes two — depending on when Easter was since we always did a stint of schoolboy coaching during the holiday period — we would have our first practice match. Traditionally this was against Halstead, which is a town on the eastern side of Essex. Their beautiful ground is in a meadow on a hill on the outskirts of the town. The pavilion has a thatched roof. There are tall fir trees on one side and the other is wired off from the park-like field beyond, where cows lazily graze.

The opposition were mostly farmers and occasionally they would import a well-known player or two to stiffen up the side. One such man had a bowling action that had brought him notoriety and a large crop of wickets. As we drove to the ground, those who batted low down the order would pull the legs of their companions higher up, who were going to have to gain their early-season confidence against the projectiles this man delivered on the never very certain Halstead pitch.

Whenever I drive past the Halstead ground I recall with pleasure those springtime games and the fun we had. Once, when Tom Pearce gave the ball to Ray Smith and asked what he was going to bowl, Ray said, 'Well, at this time of the season, skipper, I think the main thing is to try and hit the pitch.'

Provided the weather was good, it was not long before we had had enough of nets, and practice matches, and were anxious to get going on the real thing.

Our first three-day match of the season was often against

Cambridge University. It was a fixture that made a pleasant start to
the summer. One would motor up through the lovely East Anglian
countryside, wondering what fortune the day would bring. By
supper-time one might have 50, 80 or even 100 runs to one's
name, or five wickets, with the glow and promise of a bumper
season ahead. Or it might be a low score and the suspicion that this
was going to be the year all cricketers dread when nothing goes
right.

Cambridge is especially beautiful at this time of the year. The
cherry blossom is blazing, the daffodils, wallflowers, and the fresh
green of the willow trees give their spring-time dressing to the
lovely buildings.

Fenner's, the University cricket ground, is always a picture. An
artist groundsman of the highest skill was in residence there: Cyril
Coote, reputed also to be the best shot in the county. He produced
superb wickets with the ease of an Academician executing a
portrait.

I am told that when it was recently decided to build a new
pavilion at Fenner's, the suggestion was made that it should be put
in a position which would have meant moving the 'square' on
which the pitches are prepared. When Cyril was asked about this,
he is said to have replied that it would be easier to move King's
College Chapel. So the new pavilion stands in a place which enabled
Cyril's 'square' to stay put.

He and his wife prepared the meals we had in the pavilion. If one
felt one was sufficiently senior a player to approach him for his
views he would give shrewd judgments on the current crop of
cricketers at the University.

Lunches at this match were always interesting. The two teams sat
with each other. I would look at and talk to these young men and
try and foresee which would be household names in a few years' time
— men like May, Bailey, Insole, Marlar, Dexter, Sheppard.

Although so close to Essex, Cambridge was classed as an away
match, which meant we would be staying at an hotel for the first
time in the season. Sometimes we stayed at the Boar's Head and
sometimes at the University Arms. The latter adjoins the famous
Cambridge greensward, Parker's Piece, where Jack Hobbs learned
his early cricket. This stretch of turf can accommodate half-a-dozen
cricket matches. Crossing this from the hotel one comes to a small
lane off which the Fenner's ground is situated.

The feeling of the players at the end of the first day of a new season is a mixture of relief and satisfaction — a bit like after the first day of term at school. In the dressing-room after close of play, the players usually sink on to the bench where their clothes are hanging and have a drink; beer for most, soft drinks for some. Then there are the quick changers and the slow changers. But for almost all cricketers it is surprising how soon their thoughts switch from the activities of the day towards the activities of the coming night. Even the slowest changers are not all that slow, and before long all the players have made their way back to the hotel for dinner. In the dining-room sometimes a table is set aside to accommodate all the players but usually we sat three or four together at the normal ones.

Afterwards a few may spend the evening in the bar, but Essex men are keen cinema-goers. In a place like Cambridge, also, Essex players who had been at the University were entertained by old college friends.

Back at the hotel later, the players would often foregather for tea and biscuits before putting in for a not-too-early call for the morning and drifting off to bed.

Most players were good sleepers. A few put off their departure for their rooms as long as possible. Essex batsman Dick Horsfall was one of these. Dick was a big raw-boned Yorkshireman. He was a gentle giant except when it came to hitting a cricket ball, which he did with great ferocity. But his nerves did not quite match his physical strength. He smoked endlessly. Although I never shared a room with him I imagined him a restless sleeper: the sort of man who regards the bedroom with suspicion as a place where, in the dark and quiet of the early waking hours, unknown horrors and fears come in to prey on the unsleeping mind.

Our rooms were mostly of the twin-bedded variety with perhaps one or two singles. The pairings of players to share rooms was usually amicably and mutually arranged.

The pattern for most players in the mornings would be to arrive down to breakfast between 8.30 and 9, having read of their exploits of the previous day in the paper in bed over their early-morning tea.

The rule in Essex was that every player had to be on the ground an hour before play began. This meant that transport would leave the hotel sometime after ten. Between breakfast and this time the players would sit around in the lounge chatting and writing letters.

Essex also had a number of crossword addicts who would now be busily at work.

On arrival on the ground the first thing would be another cup of tea. Some would change and go for batting and bowling practice in the nets or in front of the pavilion. Others would have fielding practice. But I found that opinion varied on the value of practice before the game. One well-known player in our side said he preferred to get his runs in the match rather than in the nets.

Meanwhile the gates had been opened to the public and those spectators who wanted to obtain specially placed seats had begun to arrive.

At 11.15 a bell in the pavilion would be rung denoting that play would begin in 15 minutes. The batters would now be in their pads and gear and perhaps giving their eyes a rinse with cold water and generally exhibiting signs of tension. These signs would always indicate a visit to the toilet for what players called 'a nervous one'.

The bell would be rung again at 11.25 and the umpires would make their way down the pavilion steps and out to the middle. If Essex were fielding, the skipper would shout 'All aboard!' and make for the dressing-room door, to be followed by the senior professional, also echoing the cry, and the rest would follow. The team would generally go out in rough order of seniority. But cricketers are as superstitious as the next man and there would be players who believed that fortune favoured them, or the side, or both, if they went out third or last or whatever.

With the fielders on their way, the batsmen would follow. Again, some batsmen would be right on the heels of the fielders; others favoured a more delayed entrance to the arena.

With the players in position, the spectators in their seats, the sightscreens adjusted to everyone's satisfaction, and the inevitable stray dog captured by its owner or chased off the ground, the umpire would call play and the action began.

This was the sort of routine that was followed each day of an Essex away county match. It varied on the last day in that the game usually started at 11 am to enable the match to end earlier and make it easier for the teams to reach their next destinations.

At the end of the game at Cambridge the Essex players quickly change, pack their bags, and hurry out of the pavilion to their cars, signing autograph books of the boys who always wait to catch them at these moments. Some players would set aside time to sign the books of all those who asked. Essex wicketkeeper Paul Gibb was one of these. He would make the boys get into line and have the whole thing done in an orderly manner. Others did them on the run, or signed a few in lordly fashion from their cars before saying to the next disappointed one, 'That's all, son — I've got to go.'

We usually travelled two or three to a car. The thoughts of the players as they went would be coloured by the events of the last game. A man with a good personal performance under his belt might be more at peace with the world and his neighbour in the car than the man who had dropped two catches and had failed with bat or ball. The first would be apt to look forward to tomorrow's match; the latter would have a gnawing doubt at the back of his mind about his future which nothing but runs scored or wickets taken would alleviate.

Sometimes I have seen a bowler have a succession of matches without taking a wicket. He soon gets to the point where he thinks he is never going to get one again. And when he does, his relief is so great he breaks out into a cold sweat.

It is customary for the scorer at the end of a day's play to bring the bowling analysis into the dressing-room for the perusal of the captain of the fielding side. He may also have a copy for the senior professional. One of these may be given to a successful bowler. Essex pace bowler Ken Preston used to keep his best analysis sheets in his blazer pocket to look at on his blank days to keep his spirits up.

But talkative or pensive, the players, after a stop en route for dinner, would arrive at the next match at Nottingham, where the University Arms would be replaced by the Flying Horse.

The older hands on the county cricket circuit remember hotels, since the same ones tend to be used year after year, and they would try and make sure that their room in the Flying Horse was as far out of earshot of the town's nightlong striking clock as possible.

The routine in the morning before going to the Trent Bridge ground might be varied by a visit to the famous Gunn and Moore bat factory.

I believe most county cricketers these days get their bats free from manufacturers. This was not always so, though we did get them at a reduced rate. Some of us would always go to Gunn and Moore to see if we could find a bat that took our fancy.

Some batsmen are fussier than others over the bats they use.

When I asked Jack Russell, who had got many runs for Essex and England, what sort of bat he favoured in his generation, his reply was short and matter of fact. 'I didn't mind what sort of bat it was so long as it made runs.'

After collecting a new bat from Gunn and Moore and some fresh expectancy with it, we cross the bridge over the muddy Trent river to the ground nearby from which it takes its name.

As befits a famous Test match ground, Trent Bridge has an atmosphere of history about it. And perhaps because of Nottinghamshire marl, the wickets were, and are, very good. But not so good that they could not nurture two of the game's great fast bowlers — Larwood and Voce.

I played against Voce only in his last years, when his pace had dropped to medium. One of my outstanding memories of Trent Bridge concerns his batting. I was standing on the extra-cover boundary when he hit a ball from Ray Smith, bowling in his slower style, as far as I have seen any ball struck. It seemed to be still going up when it passed high over my head. It went over the stand and finished up in the bar of the pub beyond. This bar became the ball's final resting place — in a glass case with a plaque commemorating the feat.

After Trent Bridge, we return to Essex for a week at Valentines Park, in Ilford. Until they acquired their present permanent ground at Chelmsford, Essex played all their home matches at a series of weeks on cricket grounds that were in public parks or belonged to private clubs. It was on these grounds that Mr Castor, and his successors, would, in the days prior to the 'week', invade the ground and set up boundary fencing and temporary stands and tents and marquees. The latter would be hired by local clubs and organisations, the Mayor and Corporation, the Rotarians, the local Yacht Club.

There were also marquees for lunches for the members and players and others for liquid refreshment in both the members' and public sections. It was always a very gay sight and a refreshing contrast to the stadiums in other cities.

The wickets were apt to vary in quality. In the years immediately after the war there were still craftsmen groundsmen of the highest quality, men who had given their lives to one particular ground and could turn out wickets that were a wonder to batsmen and tested the skill and ingenuity of the bowler to the uttermost.

The wicket at Valentines Park was one of these when I first played on it. Later it altered considerably and developed one of those mysterious ridges that are the curse of cricket squares. These ridges, a slight undulation in the turf, can be very hazardous if they are anywhere near a bowler's length.

I had many memorable moments on Valentines Park. On my birthday one year I hit the first ball of the match for six. Another time I hooked a ball from Warwickshire fast bowler Tom Pritchard through the pavilion window. I got a hundred against the 1951 South Africans in our first innings. In the second innings I was hit straight between the eyes by a ball from their fast bowler Michael Melle.

In 1958 we played the New Zealanders there. I had been told they did not have a fast bowler, only Hayes, who was of medium pace. A number of friends came specially to watch me in this match. After taking guard at the beginning of the Essex innings I was surprised to see this medium-pace bowler at the end of a very long run doing physical jerks. Even so I was not duly alarmed when he came bounding up to the wicket. His first ball was a very quick bouncer. I went as usual for the hook but was late, got the ball on the splice and was caught. My watching friends had been settling themselves in their seats and looked up only to see me on my way back to the pavilion.

It was in this same game that an incident happened that I have seen only once in a cricket match. Trevor Bailey bowled one ball from so close to the stumps that his bowling hand hit the wicket. The ball went straight up in the air and came to rest in the middle of the pitch. The New Zealand batsman quickly recovered from his surprise, remembered the rules, and walked up to the ball, which he proceeded to address as if he was playing golf. He then coolly hit it to the boundary. Trevor's face was a study. He clapped his hands for the ball to be returned to him and fairly dashed back to his bowling mark. He then proceeded to pepper the offending batsman with a series of bouncers and full tosses to his head.

The routine at home matches differed slightly from matches played away. For one thing nearly all the players were living at home. I was not then married and often stayed with one of the players or with other friends. We arrived at the ground the statutory hour before play. Tea was drunk in one of the marquees. But pre-match practice was limited. While the wickets on these park grounds were adequate there were seldom any net facilities and the outfields were often too bumpy to bat on.

One of the chores all cricketers do at some time before a game is to leave tickets at the gate for their friends — or other people's friends. We used to be allowed two complimentary tickets a day, so if a player had a larger party it was a question of borrowing from players who were not using their own tickets.

Spectatorship by friends is a great art, but if friends come on the 'give' rather than on the 'get' they cannot go wrong as far as the players are concerned.

British sportsmen are often the objects of hero-worship in various degrees. There are those who like to obtain reflected glory from being seen with, or talking to , sportsmen, especially when they are doing well. This is what I mean by being on the get. After a time sportsmen instinctively know what is happening and some build up a protective wall around themselves which makes them appear cool and distant in their response to approaches.

A spectator on the give, however, is always welcome. Essex had many of these. I remember one man who kept a garage in Dagenham. It was a broken-down old place, but this man had a heart as big as a bus. He was always ready to help in any way he could by driving us to awkward places, and he invariably greeted us in the same cheerful manner whether we had made a hundred or a duck or a series of ducks. It was always revealing how many people smiled and wanted to stop for a chat when one had done well and how, after a bad match, eyes were averted or, at best, a forced pleasantry squeezed out.

However, we will suppose we have had a good week at Valentines Park. Runs have been scored, catches caught, wickets taken and at least one match won.

There were times when winning meant a bonus of a pound or two, which always added to end-of-match cheerfulness. I can honestly say for myself, and to the best of my knowledge, others too, that this bonus never made any difference to the way we played or fielded. We never tried more or less hard because of the thought of those pounds.

Our next game is at Northampton, where we sometimes stayed at the noisiest hotel in England. It no longer exists, having been demolished to make way for the main roads that made it so unbearable. It was here that I discovered that if I slept in a very noisy room I would seem to sleep deeper but wake up tired. It had a very real physical effect, as though one had been fighting the noise all night. That is why I, and so many sportsmen, like to get a quiet night's sleep if possible.

The Northamptonshire Cricket Club share their ground with the Northampton Town Football Club. It cannot claim to be one of the most beautiful in the country. The pavilion is of red brick, and red-brick terrace houses surround the ground. The wicket always looked a little rough but played very well.

Northamptonshire seemed for many years to have a permanent tenancy of the bottom of the County Championship table before the war. They did little better afterwards until F. R. Brown took over the captaincy. But if they were at times short on cricket success, they were not short on personalities.

One of these was Dennis Brookes, their distinguished opening batsman for many years. He played in a calm and dignified manner and elegant driving was a feature of his play. He managed to make the fielding side feel that to bowl a bouncer to him was an affront against decency — not to say law and order. I was not surprised to find that he became chairman of the bench of magistrates in Northampton.

Another character was Bob Clarke, a swashbuckling, rumbustious left-arm opening bowler. I remember him bowling a bouncer that almost literally parted my hair. He'd bowl his heart out all day regardless of results. Then there were two dapper Davis brothers. One was called 'Sparrow' and they both pottered round the crease while they batted like sparrows in a farmyard.

When Freddie Brown, formerly of Surrey and England, took over the captaincy, he transformed the nature of the club with his buccaneering personality and great cricketing skills, and with the importation of fine cricketers like the Australians George Tribe and Jock Livingston they became a team to be reckoned with.

Northants did not always play in the county town. Essex were entertained at Peterborough, Rushden, where the ground was enclosed by a corrugated iron fence and the wicket was surprising, and Wellingborough, where we played on my old school ground and the wicket was superb.

We will leave Northampton with them the victors and journey north to Old Trafford — the Manchester home of Lancashire.

If county cricket is thought a bit la-di-da in the south there's none of that in Lancashire. At Old Trafford more than any other ground I felt that the officials had got their priorities right as far as the players were concerned. The moment you arrived, your needs as a player were met. From the gateman's attitude and the efficient way your car was parked you sensed they realised you were there on important business. It was as though you were a surgeon arriving to carry out an operation. Everything was done to enable you to arrive at the operating-table in the best possible shape to save the patient's life. No surgeon: no operation.

In the pavilion it was the same. The facilities there, and for practices, were as the players wanted them rather than as someone thought the players ought to want them. And on the first morning of our visit a Lancashire committee man would come into the dressing-room and ask us which of Manchester's wide range of entertainments we would like to go to, and tickets would be arranged.

Old Trafford is, and looks, a famous Test match ground. The first thing a newcomer notices is its greenness, caused by Manchester's abundant rainfall. One of the troubles about the rain at Old Trafford is its predictability. As the old players sit on the pavilion balcony they will indicate the hills in the distance. If you can see them it will be fine. If they are shrouded in mist then rain will, and does, come.

We had our share of washouts but we had our good games too. One of these was when we set Lancashire to get 299 to win on the last day. Cyril Washbrook and Winston Place opened and they set off at a tremendous pace. Cyril, especially, cut our bowling to ribbons. He cut square, fine and middling. I was at third man, throwing the balls back after they whistled by me to the boundary. Then a second third man was stationed but that only meant there were two of us to throw them back. Washbrook and Place put on 148 in 65 minutes. The Lancashire crowd were naturally rapturous. None more so than two small boys behind me in the crowd.

'You'll never get them out!' they kept shouting in my ear.

'Just you wait,' I said, though without hope.

Even when Washbrook and Place were out, Lancashire continued in fine style until, as they say, they could have walked them in singles. Instead of that, panic set in, and they rushed in like men possessed, and took wild swipes, and rushed out again. Nothing seemed able to stop them committing cricket suicide, and, to our astonishment, we won the match.

As I left the ground, I found two very disconsolate little boys waiting for an autograph. They were my two friends from the terraces. They looked so glum I gave each of them a shilling to buy an ice cream.

About twenty years later I visited the National Centre for Physical Recreation at Lilleshall. The assistant warden introduced himself. 'You won't remember me,' he said. I didn't. 'You once bought me and my friend an ice cream at Old Trafford to cheer us up.'

We sometimes played Lancashire at Liverpool and Blackpool. I have two memories of Blackpool. On the first occasion there were some boys sitting on a wall behind the square-leg boundary. Pollard bowled a bouncer which I hooked low and straight at these boys. Suddenly they saw their danger and toppled off the wall backwards with their legs in the air just in time to avoid being hit.

Many years later Gordon Barker and I opened for Essex on the first morning on this ground and put on 94 in little over an hour. Essex were all out by tea time for 271. Lancashire replied with 279 for 8 declared. We made 157 in our second innings and won the match by 26 runs. It was a low-scoring game but because of the way Essex got on with it on the first day it was always going at the right pace to get a result. It made one feel that no side ought to bat beyond teatime on the first day.

Leaving Lancashire with a win, we drive back to Essex for Brentwood cricket week. The Brentwood ground must be one of the most beautiful of its kind in the country. It is surrounded by trees. On one side is a tiny white pavilion, on another is a large country house set in formal gardens. There is a gate from this garden to a small private semi-circular enclosure on the ground. Year after year I noticed an old lady sitting under a parasol in this enclosure surrounded by a few companions. One year I decided to make myself known. Her name was Mrs Hall Payne. She told me that her husband was one of the men who had raised the money to build the Canadian Pacific Railway and that much of this money had come from around Brentwood. Her husband was long since dead and she was living her last days in this magnificent house they had built.

The first year I played at Brentwood, Gloucester were the visitors, led by that great gladiator, Walter Hammond. I had never really seen him bat and was looking forward to this chance. But it was not to be. Reg Taylor, our left-arm leg-break and chinaman expert, was bowling. Hammond danced down the wicket and committed himself totally to hitting what he thought was a leg-break for six into the car park. But the leg-break was a chinaman and the immortal Wally, looking as fallible as the next man, was stumped by some yards.

Brentwood was also the setting for one of those odd happenings that occur in county cricket from time to time. An amateur batsman called Stan Eve came into the side. He played a match or two and then at Brentwood he made a brilliant 100. Watching him cut and pull and dance down the wicket to drive was a breathtaking experience. He looked a complete player, and, judged on that innings, one would have thought him a fixture in the side.

Professional cricketers, being human, began to wonder whether it was their place in the side he would be taking. But somehow Stan never repeated this afternoon's feat and after a while faded from the county scene.

It was on this ground that Northants suffered an unbelievable collapse. Essex batted first and scored 323. Peter Murray-Willis and 'Sparrow' Davis opened for Northants. They put on 96 before Davis was run out. The rest of the side scored only 10 more runs and Essex beat them by an innings.

CHAPTER 8

Men of Essex

After Brentwood week the county has no match. Sometimes during these breaks in the fixtures the players can relax and catch up with their families and the jobs at home. But there is almost always a benefit or charity match that must be played in. On the last day of this 'rest' the players have, of course, to set out for the venue of the next game.

We will use this break to consider some of the Essex men I played with.

Essex cricketers were and, I suspect, still are, great characters. In 1946 and for some years after that, Tom Pearce, 'Burly Tom', was the captain. He came by the name of 'Burly' because his figure was built on the lines of W. G. Grace in his later years.

He was a good trencherman. At lunch, while more nervous men might toy with a little meat and salad, Tom Pearce would tackle a large plateful with the remark, 'I'm building up for a big innings!'

He made a lot of runs. He was remarkably quick in the field for one of his size. Not many of his men would let him know this. Essex humour is of the variety which says to the man who has just returned from a long hard chase to the boundary, 'Where have you been? They ran five!'

Tom, unruffled and good-natured, ran a happy ship.

Our senior professional — shop steward — in those days was Peter Smith. Peter, with his military moustache and bearing, looked like a major in the Indian army. He bowled leg-breaks and googlies, and with these got more wickets for Essex than any other bowler, as well as playing for England.

Ray Smith, cousin of Peter, was of farming stock. He was dark and handsome, with a back like a ramrod. He bowled with speed and swing and was by far our best fielder. As a batsman he would perform in either agricultural or classical fashion, scoring anything between 0 and 147 according to mood.

He had three shots which I remember best. One was a cover drive of impeccable pedigree. The second was the barley mow which he applied to all off-spinners and much else beside. When it connected, the ball would go a prodigious distance — over the mayor's marquee on the midwicket boundary if there happened to be one. Then, when he did not know what to do, Ray would play the forward prod. This he did with his chin up and backside pushed out to square leg, while his bat and front foot advanced as far down the wicket as balance, with this posture, would permit.

As a bowler, I saw Ray trouble the best batsmen in England. He could swing the ball late and far, in both directions, and on his day, could be almost unplayable. One such occasion was against Notts at Ilford. Charlie Harris and Joe Hardstaff were batting. There are more stories about Charlie Harris than about most players. This day, Ray was bowling his swingers well, and Charlie was playing and missing so often that it looked as if he was batting against an invisible ball.

Suddenly Charlie got an idea. He took out his false teeth, walked over to the square-leg umpire, and asked him to hold them. This the umpire declined to do. Grumbling to himself, Charlie made his way back to take guard against Ray, who by this time was beginning to laugh. Then Charlie put his teeth in his pocket, and, baring his gums, glared down the pitch, indicating he was now ready for battle. Ray began his run but as soon as he caught sight of those bared gums he could not continue for laughing. Finally Joe Hardstaff walked down the wicket and told Charlie to 'Pack it oop!' With the teeth restored to their proper place, play continued, but Ray's bowling that day was never quite the same again.

Sonny Avery was our most cultured batsman. He was a born ball-player. He played his early cricket in the dockside streets of London's East End. He was quiet and had a keen sense of humour; also a streak of sentiment. When he batted at The Oval the time the Essex first-wicket record was made, Sonny used a bat an old Essex member had given him. He said it had belonged to his son who had now stopped playing and he hoped Sonny would use it. He did so and made 210.

Frank Rist was, I think, typical of what most people think a professional sportsman should look like and be. Frank was tall, with a superb physique. He had strong features and his complexion was of a ruddy hue that exuded health. As well as being a professional cricketer he was a professional footballer and played centre-half for Charlton Athletic when they were a First Division side.

Frank lived for both games and his memory of matches and scores and incidents was, and is, phenomenal. He was never quite a permanent member of the Essex side. He was what is known as a good servant of the club. He would keep wicket, open the innings, field anywhere or work the scoreboard with endless good-natured grace.

When he retired as a player, Essex wisely took him on as coach and he looked after, in particular, the younger players, second eleven and club and ground sides. He also did a similar job with West Ham Football Club.

The Frank Rists of life are the backbone of many county clubs. They can always be relied on to produce players at the last moment for some charity match and whenever anyone wants something done Frank would know someone who could do it if he couldn't himself.

Now his active sporting days are over he presides with his partner over the best and most successful sports shop I know.

Essex — in those days when cricketers were still divided into 'gentlemen' and 'players' — utilised the services of more 'gentlemen' than most counties. The schoolmasters, for instance, would come into the side after the term was over in July. Then there would be the university men, the most famous of whom were Trevor Bailey and Doug Insole. Another was Jack Bailey, now secretary of MCC.

Many of the amateurs who played came and went like ships in the night. They would play a game or two and we would see them no more. Two who came and stayed, and took over the club, were Trevor Bailey and Doug Insole. Trevor, after a somewhat temperamental start, went on to achieve worldwide fame as one of the game's great all-rounders. Some called him the king of stone-wallers, but may a time his defence saved Essex and England. Occasionally, another side of his batting emerged.

One day Essex were playing Lancashire at Brentwood. On the last afternoon they were set to get 232 to win in two and a quarter hours. Insole came in with me. I hit Brian Statham's first ball for four and second ball for six. 'Hey, Dick, what's going on?' said Brian. The first fifty came in 25 minutes.

Things continued merrily along until our last two and slowest batsmen, Bailey and Vigar, were at the wicket. When the final over was called Essex needed nine runs to win with six balls to go and one wicket to fall. The excitement was intense.

Hilton, the Lancashire and England slow left-arm spinner, was the bowler. Bailey faced him and the first ball received his famous forward prod. We all groaned. Then we could scarcely believe our eyes as Trevor drove the second ball straight for a magnificent six. The cheers were ecstatic. Three runs to win. Four balls to go.

The runs could now have been pushed in the singles at which Trevor was so adept. But the heady elixir of freedom seemed to be taking over and the next ball was lashed in the direction of the last. There was an astonished gasp and then the cheers mounted with the height of the ball as another six seemed certain. But no, a fielder was beneath it, shielding his eyes as he gauged its flight. The crowd were silent. Everyone realised a catch would be attempted. The batsmen ran two. The ball fell into the fielder's hands — and out again. A great shout of relief went up from the home supporters.

Three balls to go and the scores level. One run to win. Surely we should have the prod for a single now? But the intoxication of this unaccustomed abandon was complete. There followed another drive at the next ball and again it was in the air. This time the fielder made no mistake. The game was tied.

Back in the tiny Brentwood pavilion, as the excitement subsided, there were slight remonstrations with the batsman on the nature of his final stroke. For once, Trevor, known even then for his ready analytical diagnosis, was at a loss for words.

Doug Insole was born and brought up on the Essex side of London and has the quickness of tongue and wit coupled with warmth of heart native to that part of the world. As a cricketer and footballer he was a born fighter.

His batting technique was so unusual that when he went along to the Cambridge University nets for a trial, the professional on duty took one look at him and advised the University captain to send him away. Two weeks later, a chance vacancy occurred in the Varsity side, and Insole, who in the meantime had scored a lot of runs in other matches, was invited to play. The opponents were Yorkshire. Insole got 44. A few weeks later he scored 161 not out against Hampshire. A new star had risen.

I would describe Insole as a 'do it yourself' cricketer. He was the only man I knew who used to play forward with his back foot. His most remarkable shot was one he played to a good-length ball pitching outside the off stump. He would despatch it with unerring accuracy off the face of the bat to the fine-leg boundary.

Naturally, this tended to upset the bowler — none more so than Reg Perks, who for so long led the Worcestershire attack. Reg was known as the Bishop, both for his rather pontifical figure and his fine regard for what was proper on the cricket field. One thing definitely not proper was for a young man from Cambridge to hit Perks's best and fastest outswinger down to fine leg for four.

He would stand aghast, hands on hips, and glare down the pitch. Then, snatching at the returned ball, he would rush in and let go an even faster delivery only to see the same thing happen again. I always felt Reg looked on this as the worst sort of blasphemy, and so sure was he that the perpetrator would rapidly reap the just reward of his sin, he would keep on bowling, only to take the most fearful hammering. Insole was a prolific scorer against Worcestershire.

Insole is a man of many parts. The way he drove his car made me think he had missed his real vocation: a Grand Prix racing driver. After a while, I was one of the few in our side who would travel as his passenger. He used to say, 'I like having Dickie with me. He prays while I drive'.

He would drive his car as fast as it would go without tipping over. Not only that, but as we set off, he would stop at the first fruit shop and buy a bag of apples, bananas, plums, grapes, pears, and oranges, and would proceed to eat these while he drove. One hand would be on the wheel while the other stuffed the fruit into his mouth. Pips, stones, and peel would fly out of the window as we careered along, passing everything. If we came across a column of cars, Insole would take it as a personal challenge, and work his way up the line one by one, or four at a time, till we were in front. Then we would tear off till we came to the next obstacle.

Yet, all the same, he was a bundle of nerves. He would chew his nails down to the quick. Also, on the few times when we got into trouble and there would seem no way out, he would let go the steering-wheel and grab hold of me. We never had a smash. I said he would probably only have one, and that would finish everything. However, I learned by experience to have great respect for his skill at the wheel, as in many other things.

Another side of Doug Insole's character was displayed one day when we approached Warwickshire's ground at Edgbaston. We were driving down a hill close to the ground when Doug spotted two small boys. One was in tears as he feverishly searched his pockets, while the other stood anxiously watching. Insole sized up the situation in a glance and drew up saying, 'I bet he's lost his entrance money.' The transfer of a small sum from Insole's pocket to the hand of the small boy ended a minor tragedy and made possible a day's happiness for two.

One Saturday in late winter, I was in London doing the dishes after lunch. I had the radio on, with a commentary on the Amateur Cup Final. Bishop Auckland were playing the Corinthian Casuals and I heard that Doug Insole was playing for the latter.

I left forthwith and drove out to Wembley, walking into the ground exactly behind the point where Doug was taking a corner kick. He slashed over a perfect inswinger and the ball would have gone clean into the goal had not the goalkeeper just managed to tip it over the bar for another corner. Doug took the kick again and did exactly the same thing. This time the 'keeper was beaten and the ball went in. It was a typical Insole exploit.

Doug Insole followed Tom Pearce as Essex captain. Playing cricket under both was an enjoyable experience.

A good antidote to the speed at which Doug Insole drove was a journey with the Essex wicketkeeper, Paul Gibb. Paul looked like a don. He was in fact a Cambridge graduate before playing first for Yorkshire and later becoming a professional with Essex.

Despite sparse proportions he had the largest appetite of any man I knew, especially for ice cream. During the war he had piloted Sunderland flying-boats. Some people thought he chose these craft because they were equipped with a galley.

He played his first game for Yorkshire against Nottinghamshire when Larwood and Voce were in full cry for the latter county and scored 157 not out. It would be interesting to discover how many players made their debut against Notts during the heydey of those two bowlers. The story I heard was that some regular players had a habit of discovering an injury just before the Notts match.

Shortly after Paul started playing for Essex he bought a small Ford van. He carried many of his belongings in this and sometimes even slept in it. It was not the fastest thing on the road. Moreover in those days there was a speed limit of 30 mph for commercial vehicles.

Paul would start his journeys as if back in his piloting days. He would first walk round the van carrying out a general inspection and making sure the tyres were right and the back door was locked. Then he would carefully clean the windscreen with a special cloth. This, and a check on the oil and water completed, he would climb into the driving seat, settling himself as though wriggling into the cockpit. An instrument check on the Ford dashboard of three knobs and a petrol indicator would follow. Then he would put his hands on the wheel and feet on the pedals and give them all a waggle to make sure they worked. At last the starter was pressed to bring all four cylinders bursting into life, and with the imaginary floats away he would trundle off.

It fell to my lot to travel with him on the night of Coronation Day in 1953 from Ilford to Llanelli in Wales. It would not be a small journey today even with the motorways and a fast car. In Paul's van it was an epic.

Sometime after midnight we were snaking our way round the Welsh mountains among the sheep, lost. Celebratory beacon bonfires were alight on the topmost summits. By the time we hit Llanelli and rolled into bed it was getting on for dawn.

As luck would have it we lost the toss next day and we spent the whole day in the field!

CHAPTER 9

County Round: June-July

After our few days off we drive down to Taunton to meet Somerset.

It was always a strange experience for me to stay in the County Hotel in Taunton for it was in the ballroom of this hotel that I slept for a considerable time during the war — on straw mattresses on the floor. And what is now the car park echoed with the shouts of drill sergeants.

The Somerset county cricket ground at Taunton might be described as intimate. Perhaps this is because on one side there is a high white-painted wooden wall which turns the ground in on itself. Another side is bounded by a churchyard and it was into this that Somerset's big hitter — Arthur Wellard — liked to hoist his sixes.

It was a pleasure to play against Somerset's opening batsman, Harold Gimblett. He was a creative artist. I shall always remember one shot he made against us. It was a wettish wicket and he hit a good-length straight ball from one of our fast bowlers, on the up, and sent it for six over the midwicket boundary.

'That's a shot I carry round with me in my bag,' he said. Gimblett always talked while he batted.

He made a spectacular debut against Essex at Frome. Essex heard that Somerset had this new batsman who played for a village called Watchet. When he came in, Somerset were 107 for 6, and the Essex players might have been excused for thinking that their time in the field was almost at an end. Gimblett, showing the utmost confidence from the first ball, proceeded to hit the Essex bowlers with flowing and unexpected shots to all parts of the field. His first fifty came in 29 minutes and his century in 63, which was the fastest of that season.

The story is told of how Essex batsman Jim Cutmore gave fast bowler Stan Nichols a stream of advice as to how he could get Gimblett's wicket. 'Bowl him your slower ball, Stan. Bowl him your slower ball,' he kept saying.

Finally in desperation Stan did as he was bid. Gimblett put his foot down the wicket and hit the ball out of the ground and practically back to Watchet. Nichols turned to Cutmore, 'OK, Jim,' he said, 'I've bowled him my slower one — now you go and bloodywell fetch it back.'

We will leave Somerset for our next game against Glamorgan. Playing Glamorgan is not so much like playing a county as playing a country. It is the pride of Wales that is the opposition when one crosses the River Wye.

While Cardiff Arms Park is Glamorgan's cricketing headquarters we always got the impression we played all over the southern half of the Principality. Newport; Ebbw Vale; Pontypridd; Llanelli; we visited each of them in my time.

'Passionate' is the quality I would say marked Welsh cricket. You never had a dull match. Even if the cricket got dull this would stoke up the fires in the bellies of the Welsh dragons in the dressing-room. The chief dragon had the name of Wilfred Wooller and one would be aware of smoke fuming from his nostrils to be followed shortly after by a fleck of flame, and some sudden and outrageous deed would raise the passions of performers and spectators alike.

Wilf Wooller has been the stormy life and soul of Welsh cricket for a generation, as player, captain, secretary, and father confessor. The stories about him are legion. I will tell only one.

He and I had a crackling relationship. He was the opening bowler to my opening batsmanship on many occasions. One such time was at Ebbw Vale, where the ground nestles into one side of an old slag-heap, now overgrown with grass. Opposite is a sizable brook and although there is wire netting to prevent the ball taking a dip when hit in that direction there is a limit to its height. On this particular day I was lobbing Wilf's inswingers into this brook and the new ball was beginning to look bedraggled. Suddenly Wilf glowered down the wicket. 'If that's what comes of going to church,' he said, 'I'll go myself next Sunday.'

No matter what the state of the game if the 'hwyl' gets into the crowd and the Welsh players you never know what is going to happen next and the impossible is often accomplished. Just such a happening took place at Ebbw Vale in 1949 when Essex set

Glamorgan to get 177 to win in 105 minutes. With Trevor Bailey in our side, who certainly had more tricks for slowing down the scoring rate than anyone else I knew, the idea that we might be beaten scarcely crossed our minds.

I was fielding on the boundary for most of the ensuing 75 minutes it took Glamorgan to win. Phil Clift was the main executioner. He had the 'hwyl' all right. He just took off to inspired heights and cut, drove, and snicked runs to improbable places at an unstoppable rate. The crowd were in such a state of emotion that I moved several yards inside the boundary in case they decided to finish us off as well as the match.

The story is also told of a game at Ebbw Vale when a mist rolled down the mountains so that play was held up. Indeed it became so dense that the whole ground was blotted out. When the wind blew the mist away it was discovered that the mist was not the only thing that had come down the mountain. The ground was covered with sheep.

From Glamorgan to Derby is a long haul — but county cricketers have to learn to take such journeys in their stride.

Any batsman going to play against Derby tends to think of fast bowlers and the advisability of wearing a good thick thigh-pad. Even rib-protectors in the eras of some bowlers, like Bill Copson and 'Big Les' Jackson, would have been handy to have. Bowlers, of course, have in mind the harvest they may reap on the green wickets that Derby possesses.

Derbyshire never seem to go in much for batsmen — their strength was always their fast bowlers. As well as the blood-and-guts variety, they also had the genuine seam and swing men of gentler pace. George Pope was one of these and so, later, was Cliff Gladwin.

Cliff used to bowl huge banana-shaped inswingers. He also was said to have a computer-like brain that worked out his bowling average to several decimal points after each ball he sent down.

Once I invented a novel way of playing these boomerang balls which resulted in their being despatched to the square-leg boundary with some success. However, I was not able to develop my theory, as Cliff suddenly strained a muscle and had to go off.

One year we played Derby at Buxton when not a ball was bowled for three days because of rain. What do county cricketers do if it rains? Well if you are in Buxton you don't do much. The cards may come out. There is much hanging about the pavilion. If the rain is heavy, the match often gets abandoned for the day early and one can get off to the cinema if one is playing away, or go home if one is in Essex.

In Buxton it not only rained, the whole place seemed to exist in a cloud. When it was not actually raining some of us tried our hand at bowls on a rink that adjoined the pavilion. We were also graced by the presence of the 11th Duke of Devonshire during this fixture. He offered to take some of us over to Chatsworth and show us his magnificent stately home. I think only four of us accepted his invitation but the others missed a memory that will last long after that of the day's play we might have had if it had been fine.

But wet days at cricket matches are wretched things. True there is sometimes a moment in late July and August when one longingly looks towards the known rainy quarter of a ground to see what hope there may be of a rest for which jaded spirits and a weary body long. But usually when rain comes and really spoils the tempo of a match it is a relief when the umpires or captains make a final inspection of the pitch and signal towards the dressing-room that it is all over. There is then a rush to pack and get away and start with a fresh match, and a fine day, on another ground.

While we have been in Buxton the ground at Westcliff-on-Sea has been prepared. Westcliff-on-Sea might more truthfully be called Westcliff-on-Estuary for it is the ships moving up to Tilbury and London on the Thames Estuary that can be seen sometimes as one is fielding on the Westcliff ground. The Kent coast is also clearly visible on the other side.

One of the features of Westcliff week was the catering. Cricketers enjoy good food. It is the fuel that fires their boilers. The catering at Westcliff was done by the firm of Garrons. Mr Garron was always in evidence and his complexion and build were ample witness to the excellence of his fare. If only because of the food I think it is true to say that all counties liked playing in Essex, for the other main caterers, Whites, were no slouches either. In fact there was healthy competition.

The wicket at Westcliff could be very good and sometimes very poor. Of course, being a seaside wicket, there was always the story that the ball would begin to move more off the seam when the tide came in. The theory was that the incoming tide somehow resulted in moisture getting into the turf and 'greening' it up, which helped

the ball move more off the seam. At any rate on seaside grounds one
might be batting on a plumb pitch for the first half of the day and
then, in the middle of the afternoon, the ball would suddenly start
to move. Although it was a theory widely held I never met a captain
who studied the tides and planned his strategy accordingly.

It was at Westcliff that I took a wicket with my first ball in county
cricket. We were short of pace bowlers and for some days prior to
this game I had been endangering the shins of my colleagues during
practices in front of pavilions with balls delivered with a sort of
whippy sling. These colleagues succeeded in persuading our skipper,
Tom Pearce, to give me a go. When he threw me the ball I had not
even measured out, or practised, a fast bowler's run. However,
while the skipper set the field, I paced out a run which I hoped was
impressively long. Meanwhile the field placing had been completed,
with the exception of Frank Rist. 'Where shall I go, skipper?' asked
Frank. 'Go where you ruddy well like,' he growled. So Frank stood
where he was — somewhere in no man's land on the leg side. I ran
in at speed. Jack Robertson, the prolific and cultured Middlesex and
England batsman, faced me down the wicket. Unfortunately I was
thinking so hard about my spectacular run-up that I paid little
attention to the ball's destination and, in fact, it went straight at
Jack Robertson's head. Picking it up late, he hastily lifted his bat to
protect himself and the ball lobbed of it in the air and it was caught
by Frank Rist standing by such happy chance in just the right place.

It was also at Westcliff that I had about my only experience of
being dropped or 'rested' from the side. It is an experience that is
doubtless good for the soul though I found it somewhat painful. For
instance, do you hope your replacement does well or badly? You
know what you should feel, but are keenly aware that you don't.

In the event I was out of the team for only one match and so after
my 'rest' we travel up to what many regard as the heart of
cricketdom — Yorkshire.

There have been years when it was a major news story for
Yorkshire not to win the County Championship. Cricket-minded
Yorkshiremen (are there any other sort?) tend to regard themselves
and their county as the repository of all truth and wisdom as far as
the game is concerned and in their eyes there are no players like
Yorkshire players.

It is a fact that any match against Yorkshire is a tough match.
There is, for a start, the psychological barrier to break through.

When you go in to bat against Yorkshire, their players do their best to make you feel a second-class citizen and that you really have quite a nerve even to consider yourself good enough to play against them. The respectful and proper thing to do would be to give yourself up with all speed and return to the pavilion.

The truth is that Yorkshire seem to have an inexhaustible supply of fine players. Other counties are peppered with their discards. You still have to be born in Yorkshire to play for Yorkshire. This is not the case in any other county.

But Essex had a trump card to play with all Yorkshiremen. It was dealt long ago in Huddersfield. Yorkshire supporters who arrived an hour or so after play began on the first day of this match found that Essex were batting and apparently making very heavy weather of the Yorkshire attack, their score was so low. Then they learned the unbelievable had happened. Essex were the second side to bat that morning. Their favourite sons had already been shot out in an hour for 31. Essex went on to score 334. Yorkshire, still bemused, made only 99 second time round. This all happened when the county were at the height of their fame and in a season when, up to that time, they were unbeaten.

The first match I played against Yorkshire was at Harrogate. Paul Gibb was standing in as captain for the match. He spent most of the time a lonely and silent figure at deep fine leg. A sort of shop stewards' committee ran the show headed by Arthur Wood and Frank Smailes. There was also plenty of gratuitous advice and comment from the rank and file.

Yorkshire entertained us all over the county, and on many of these grounds we could witness the debut of one of their new players. That time at Harrogate it was the turn of a young man called Smithson. He batted quite well and then got out when he shouldn't. The older Yorkshire players took him severely to task. Yorkshire later discarded him and he went to Leicester.

Then one year we went to Middlesbrough and Don Wilson came on the scene. I was batting when he came on to bowl his first over for Yorkshire and I hit his first two balls for four. The critical Yorkshire crowd were just beginning a rumble of discontent when his third delivery got me out. Don went on to have a distinguished career and played for England.

Travelling up by train for one match I met the great Yorkshire opening bat Herbert Sutcliffe in the corridor. He began to tell me of a new fast-bowling find they had who was playing against us the next day. Herbert hinted that he was pretty quick. I passed this intelligence on to my opening partner Sonny Avery. Essex batted first on the morrow and Sonny and I watched the Yorkshire side file past our dressing-room door, waiting for our first sight of this new speed man. When he came he was so tall his head was almost hidden by the doorway. We looked at each other and there was a nervous chuckle.

However, despite his size he was not particularly fast. His name was McHugh and he seemed fated not to have a career with Yorkshire. Sonny and I both snicked him and were dropped and he did not have a successful debut. Later he joined Gloucestershire but was dogged by ill-luck.

I remember playing Yorkshire at Scarborough, Bradford, Leeds, and Sheffield. On these grounds we watched the copperplate batting of the master, Len Hutton. We were bamboozled by the bowling of Bob Appleyard during his brief but brilliant career. We observed the rise of Fiery Fred Trueman, and, one afternoon at Bradford, I joined the long line of those who have had the privilege of being hit on the head by his bouncer. We were often the victims as honest Vic Wilson put his large leg down the wicket and bludgeoned our bowling with blacksmith blows. Brian Close also displayed his prodigal talents before us before he left to join Somerset. As an 18-year-old colt he took five Essex wickets and scored 88 not out in only his fifth county game.

One always leaves Yorkshire with the sense of having been in a hard match and with the knowledge that whoever are one's next opponents the game will be just that little bit easier. Before we do so I would add that there was one main difference between cricket pavilions in Yorkshire and those in the south. The Yorkshire ones were equipped with fireplaces and usually the fires were lit and were extremely welcome.

Now we come back down the A1 and enter the quite different atmosphere of Kent.

Kent, like Essex, play all over this county of hopfields and orchards. I first played them on the Mote ground at Maidstone, which was a delight, with tents and marquees and cars on the ground from which the occupants could watch, and a very good wicket.

This was in the days of Todd and Arthur Fagg and also Doug

Wright. Les Ames was still playing as a batsman, and keeping wicket was a young man called Godfrey Evans, who was beginning to get a lot of wickets with his stumping and catching and talking behind the wicket.

We seemed to be Arthur Fagg's favourite side. It was true that some batsmen always scored runs against certain counties. We were Arthur's county. Once he rather hogged his luck by scoring two double-centuries in the same match against Essex, a unique performance. But although when I saw him he was in the autumn of his career, his method — and especially his hooking — was much to be admired.

Les Todd always gave me the impression that there was a grudge just around the corner in his life. He certainly had a grudge one day when he hit a ball with unexpected abandon at the Mote and I ran a long way and just as unexpectedly caught it at full stretch, falling into the crowd. Rightly he felt himself hard done by.

Kent never appeared able to find any opening bowlers of speed. Wicketkeepers grew on trees. They bred pedigree spin bowlers. But for some reason, until Fred Ridgway began to work up a bit of pace, there was nothing to fear in this line on Kentish grounds.

I always enjoyed watching and playing against the leg-spinners and googlies of Doug Wright because of his unexpectedness. He might bowl a double-bouncer or a virtually unplayable ball, or anything in between, and he did it all with tremendous grace and artistry. Doug was an interesting character to talk to and, in my view, he has written one of the best books for boys on coaching.

Kent have other lovely grounds besides the Mote; Canterbury, of course, and Tunbridge Wells were two we played on. I never played at Dover or Folkestone. Most often we had to play at Gravesend, Dartford or Blackheath for commercial reasons. It was thought that because these places were nearest to Essex the attendances would be larger.

I remember once at Blackheath the game had reached a moribund state. It often did at Blackheath, where the wicket was too good. In this match Dick Horsfall and I were batting out the final minutes of the game, which was hopelessly drawn. The last ball of the day came up. Dick at the bowler's end decided he had achieved a 'not out' innings, with the resulting .slight increase in his batting average. He was using his bat-handle as a sort of shooting-stick as the bowler ran in to deliver this final ball to me. I played it into the covers and called for a quick single. I shall never forget the startled look on Dick's face as he grappled with the situation in his mind and then pulled himself together and launched off, to scramble in by a hairsbreadth. Anyway it livened up the proceedings and sent the spectators off home laughing and chattering like sparrows in a cornfield.

I suppose one could say that Frank Woolley is the patron saint of Kentish cricket. He was one of my boyhood heroes. I always looked for his scores in the paper and revelled in the cricket-writers' praise of his innings. I never had the luck to see him make any runs, although I twice made a special journey to do so. The first was when I was still at school. I was desperately disappointed to find he was out by the time we got to the ground. I made the mistake of expressing my disappointment when I had the chance to speak to him. His reply was a model of graciousness and modesty. 'Oh, never mind,' he said, 'Les Ames and Todd are still in and they are very good players.'

The second occasion was some early wartime match at Lord's. The wicket was wet when the great man came in. There was one graceful arc of the bat as he went to drive. The ball must have stopped a little and he was caught off an enormous skier for nought.

Having read of Frank Woolley's skill as a hooker of fast bowling I asked him, when I was having trouble with bouncers, what his secret was. His technical reply has gone from my mind. I then asked him the question that was really on my mind. 'What did you do if you were afraid?'

'You must never be afraid,' he said, as if fear were like baggage that could be discarded as not wanted, or needed, on a batting journey.

No visit to Kent would be complete without some delicate touches from Colin Cowdrey. Cuts executed with a sudden deft certainty that brings a gasp of delight from spectators. Similar deflections to leg, as opposed to the snicks of more ordinary mortals, and, in between, the stature of the man would be revealed as he leant into a ball on the off and hit it with a full imperious swing of his bat to the boundary.

Leaving Kent, we drive through the Dartford Tunnel to Colchester, which proudly claims to be the oldest town in the Kingdom.

By now it is high summer. The walk through the castle grounds on the way to the cricket is something to be done at leisure and savoured. The roses for which Colchester is famous are abloom. As you pause in the shade of the trees beside the castle walls you can read a plaque which says that it was on that spot that the two Royalist captains, Sir Charles Lucas and Sir George Lisle, were executed by firing squad by Cromwell's men for defending the castle in the King's cause.

Further down the hill one passes through a gap in the wall built around the town by the Romans. And there below, on the other side of the river, is the county ground with all its tents, set out among the willow trees. It looks a picture, and Colchester was always one of my favourite cricket weeks. The wickets were good and because it was so low-lying, there was always some moisture in the outfield making it easy on the feet in the driest weather.

Success and failure came my way at Colchester. While getting runs against Derbyshire's Les Jackson I thought how different it was playing against him on the urbane pitch as opposed to dicing with his bowling on the greasy wickets in Derbyshire. I remember a hundred against Warwickshire, and getting bowled out first ball by one of the best deliveries I ever had, sent down by Surrey's Peter Loader. Against Middlesex, I hooked Alan Moss for six in the first over of the game. The ball went a great distance and finished up under the wooden platform on which the pavilion stands. When it was recovered five minutes later the ball was considerably the worse for wear. Denis Compton came up to me while it was being found, asking to look at my bat and trying to find out why it had sent the ball so far.

It was at Colchester that I played what was to be my last innings for Essex. Yorkshire were our opponents and, strangely, Essex were top of the Championship table when the match started.

After our week there this time we will drive across the country to play against Gloucestershire, the home of the father of cricket — W. G. Grace.

The Bristol ground, where Grace and Hammond, not to mention Charlie Barnett and Tom Goddard, batted and bowled, is unexpected. If red brick is the dominant building material surrounding the ground at Northampton, in Bristol it is grey stone. Along one side of the ground a long institutional-looking structure is built of it. So are the houses at the back of the stone pavilion. Opposite the pavilion one has the impression of open country, as

beyond the boundary there is another ground. The wicket was also
unexpected. It had a lifeless quality and was apt to crumble. The ball
tended to keep low and I was forever trying to hook long hops that
hit my pads shin-high.

But there were some great Gloucester characters. I was able to
watch the last seasons of Charlie Barnett's exhilarating batting.
No-one who saw him will forget Tom Goddard, lantern-jawed and
gravel-voiced, wheeling away with his off-spinners. He took 238
wickets with them in 1947 in his 47th year.

I remember Tom Graveney and his brother, Ken, coming on the
scene. We were playing Gloucestershire on the Cheltenham ground.
At lunch the Mayor of Cheltenham launched into a long speech in
praise of what he called the Gravenitt brothers. His eloquence so
carried him away that we were late for the restart.

George Lambert was their fast bowler for many years. A great
servant of the club — he must have been one of the best county fast
bowlers never to play for England.

Gloucestershire had some colourful captains. One of these was Sir
Derrick Bailey, son of a South African diamond millionaire. He was
not the best player in the world but courage, together with a
straight bat on the forward push, once got him a hundred in county
cricket.

B. O. Allen captained them for many years. When one of Essex's
swing bowlers was bending balls like a boomerang and having some
difficulty in controlling them so that they homed on to the wicket
where Allen was batting, he called out, 'Say, are you bowling in
the same parish as I am batting?'

Once at Bristol we had to get the last batsman out in the final
over to win. By some unexpected stroke of genius the captain had
got me bowling my leg-breaks. These had no effect and finally I
decided to stake everything on my highly erratic and unpredictable
googly. The great art of bowling a googly is that it should look
exactly like a leg-break in the way it is delivered, but, of course, it
turns from the opposite direction. Some bowlers are more skilled
than others in this difficult art. Doug Insole used to say jokingly
that when our leg-spin expert bowled his googly it was so obvious
that the band would stand up and play *God Save the King*. Anyway,
I ran up and slipped my googly. Wonder of wonders it pitched a
length; the batsman by some aberration thought it was a leg-break,
got a faint touch, and was caught at the wicket, and the match was
won.

CHAPTER 10

County Round: August-September

Our next game is at Worcester. For years we played them on either August or Whitsun Bank Holiday. The August match always coincided with the Conservative fete which was held in the field next to Worcester's lovely Cathedral-dominated ground. In the afternoon the fielding side would be regaled with the feats of the Conservatives by the local Member of Parliament over a loud-speaker system designed to carry the length of the county.

It was all rather counter-productive as far as we were concerned as, in addition to the high decibels, the speaker had a voice that sounded as though it was stuffed with Worcester plums. He would end by calling on everyone to return him and the Conservatives at the next election with 'a thumping great majority'. We tended to have decided to vote for something else by the time he had finished.

Election meetings apart, playing at Worcester is no hardship. It is undeniably a beautiful ground, with its Cathedral, river, chestnut and lime tree setting. In the mind of memory the sun was always shining at Worcester, with the grass beautifully mown in broad swathes and a wicket which if you were a batsman you enjoyed — and even for a bowler there was hope.

We would stay at the Star or the Diglis by the river. It was at about this time of the season, after three months' travelling and playing, that one was apt to wake up in the morning and wonder where one was. Players might also take stock of their season's work. The batsman would have his eye on his thousand or fifteen-hundred runs, and the bowler on his target of a hundred wickets.

We leave Worcester and drive through the Vale of Evesham, where the fruit in the órchards is beginning to ripen, and pass round London on the North Circular Road on our way to Southend-on-Sea. Southend is a bit further down the Thames estuary from Westcliff and there is no place quite like it. Its daytime population has mostly come on a day trip from the East End of London. Mums, some dads, and masses of children.

Southend has every form of sideshow along its front to delight a child. It has a mile-long pier with a very necessary railway to take you to its end. When the tide is out there is a mile or more of mud before you find the water. The mud has an odour said to be invigorating.

I first met Sir Leonard Hutton late one night before the Yorkshire game at Southend. He was in confidential mood and asked me — as one opening batsman to another, which flattered me no end — how you played a fast short ball coming at your ribs. I think it was a bit on his mind as he had spent the previous winter in Australia, where he had had plenty from Lindwall and Miller.

It was in this same match that I got a chance to field in the slips and promptly dropped Hutton before he had scored. He went on to make 197. I never got the chance to field much in the slips after that.

Before the 75-yard limit was introduced, Southend had a very long boundary on one side. This was brought home painfully to me when the Australians scored 721 runs against us in a day. I spent most of that time on this long boundary throwing the balls back. 721 is a lot of runs, but in fact it only worked out at a scoring rate of eight runs, or two boundaries, an over.

The one batsman who did not score was Keith Miller. He came in looking thoroughly bored with the run feast and made little attempt to play the first ball he received, which bowled him. He sauntered out with his bat over his shoulder and according to legend went off to the races. True or not, we spent the day racing round the boundary. Frank Vigar was put on for the last over before lunch to try his leg-breaks against Bradman. Bradman's idea of playing safe for the lunch interval was to hit him for five fours.

Funnily enough we were the only county to get the Australians all out in a day during the summer.

An innings which gave me great satisfaction at Southend was a century against the West Indian side in which Sonny Ramadhin played. This was the first of his visits to Britain and he played havoc with the best of English batting with his unorthodox spin.

I had taken the precaution of asking two batsmen who made runs against Ramadhin what their secret was. The great thing appeared to be not to lose one's nerve if, by the time the ball was on its way, one had not the slightest idea which way it was going to turn. I was glad of this innings since many used to say I could not play spin bowling — a view not shared by myself. It was true that after dicing with the speed men I was often so relieved when the soft stuff came on that there was a momentary lapse of concentration that was fatal.

One year a brewery set up a tented inn just behind the square-leg boundary. I happened to hook a ball for six and it went straight into the bar of this inn and knocked out both barmaids. It appeared the ball hit the beer pump and ricocheted on to the head of barmaid one who collapsed. It then went on to the head of barmaid two, who also collapsed. When my wife heard this story, she, like many others, thought it rather far-fetched, so I was glad when I was able to introduce her to one of the victims, who confirmed its truth and even spoke of the incident with pride.

In another match against Yorkshire we had Charlie Williams, the Oxford University captain, playing for us. He wore his colourful Harlequin cap for the occasion. This was a dangerous thing to do when Fred Trueman was in the opposition, for Fred was known to regard what he called 'fancy caps' in the same way that a bull regards a red rag. However, Charlie was no slouch with the bat and he not only stood up to Fred's fire but he had the temerity to hit him straight for four. As the ball was on its way and Charlie was going through the motions of running the first run he passed Fred snorting at the end of his followthrough. 'Well, lad,' said Fred, 'tha knows what to expect.' 'Yes,' said Charlie, 'a bouncer.' 'Aye,' said Fred, 'but just dook and tha'll be all right.' Fred bowled his ritual bouncer. Charlie ducked and honour was served.

There was an interesting match against Warwickshire at Southend. Warwickshire batted first and made 284. Essex were something like 80 for 7 at the close of the first day's play. There was talk of the game being over in two days with Warwickshire winning by an innings. The game was over in two days but with Essex winning by an innings. D. R. Wilcox got 134, and Reg Taylor 142, and Essex were all out for 385 and bowled Warwickshire out in their second innings for 81.

During this Southend week, players might notice that longer shadows are beginning to be cast by the late afternoon sun and they have the first sense that the end of the season is in sight. Most professionals are on a yearly contract. By now the committee have met and decided which contracts are to be renewed.

A professional cricketer's life is in every way insecure. A serious injury can end it any day. The condition of employment is the making of runs or the taking of wickets. These are a player's security.

But we will suppose that our contract for another season is secure and with this comforting thought tucked away in the back of our minds we leave Southend for the next game against Warwickshire at their Edgbaston ground in Birmingham.

The magnificent Edgbaston stadium is largely the creation of their secretary, Leslie Deakins. I am told that while serving in the navy in the war he used to dream of transforming the Warwickshire ground and he has turned his dream into a reality.

In addition to his administrative ability I have always found Mr Deakins to be a most thoughtful and considerate man. During the first years of my career my father was still living in his parish of Hatton, and when we played against Warwickshire Mr Deakins would arrange for him to come and watch from the committee box as a guest of the club. It was a gesture my father very much appreciated, though I am not sure he saw me make many runs there.

The crowd at Birmingham was small but vocal. They could not abide Trevor Bailey, who used to bait them. I once saw Trevor contrive to bowl the longest over I have ever witnessed. First he missed his run-up. Slight reaction from the crowd. Then, as he was running in again to bowl, he got a fly in his eye and stopped to deal with it. More reaction. Then on his next approach to the bowling crease he decided his bootlace needed re-tying and it turned out to be a complicated operation. By this time the crowd were fairly baying for his blood. Then Trevor sat down and refused to bowl till they shut up. It all added to the interest.

Warwickshire have been fortunate in their captains. They pioneered the way with a professional captain in the person of Tom Dollery, under whom they won the County Championship in 1951. Then there were the two Smiths, M. J. K. and A. C. These men will have helped to keep together a team gathered from often far beyond the county's boundaries. Someone said that playing Warwickshire was like playing against the United Nations.

The last Midland county we visit is Leicestershire, who play at their Grace Road ground and headquarters in Leicester. This is a

My father

*Myself in front of the Warwick School
pavilion after making a hundred*

*Playing forward, aged about six, on the vicar-
age lawn at Riseley*

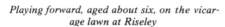

My son, Michael, in the nets at our home

Services XI v Indian XI 1944. My first major match. Back row: Capt R. G. Hunt, Capt H. G. King, Sgt Dobrey Carey, Lt H. R. Adhikari, Gnr S. Cray, Pte Stansfield, Sgt H. J. Butler; front row: Capt T. C. Dodds, Capt A. G. Skinner, Major D. R. Jardine (capt), BSM J. Hardstaff, Capt Mohamed Saeed

My last first-class match — MCC v Scotland. Back row: A. L. Dixon, W. B. Bridge, J. D. Bannister, A. Brown, P. H. Jones, J. F. Harvey; front row: D. G. Ufton, A. H. Phebey, T. C. Dodds (capt), J. K. Hall, R. C. Wilson

In Burma, 1944, with a Chinthe — the mythical animal that guards the Buddhist temples

Sitting in the deckchair and on the spot where I decided to change, 1946. The gramophone travelled the length of Burma

Essex XI in 1947. Back row, left to right: Dickie Dodds, Frank Vigar, Ray Smith, Tom Wade, Chick Cray, Dick Horsfall; front: Peter Smith, Doug Insole, Tom Pearce (capt), Denys Wilcox, Harry Crabtree, Trevor Bailey

*Ray Smith demonstrates his
classic swing bowler's action*

Doug Insole forcing a ball against Surrey

*Trevor Bailey and Brian Taylor successfully appealing for a catch off the bowling of Jack
Bailey to dismiss Richie Benaud*

Hooking a ball from Stuart Surridge, Surrey. He and I had many tussles

Hitting out against South Africa at Ilford, 1951. I scored 138

Opening the Essex innings with Sonny Avery against Kent at Valentine's Park, Ilford, in 1949

With Conrad Hunte, the West Indian cricketer, during a Moral-Re-Armament tour of Australia in 1965. We are talking with Les Stuart (right) and Jim Beggs, secretary and vice-president respectively of the Melbourne Branch of the Waterside Workers Federation

Queuing to get in to my benefit match

*Tod Sloan, East End revolutionary and friend of Keir Hardie, comes to my benefit match
— his last outing*

Major American League baseball player Jack
Phillips and English county cricketer Dickie
Dodds exchange bat and ball. My acquisition
was called a 'Genuine Louisville Slugger'

Match at St Mark's, Kennington Ova
Bridesmaids from Ghana, South Africa
Japan, Pakistan and Britain

*Sonny and Marjorie Avery watch a lively conversation, after our wedding, between (left to
right) Roger Hicks, author; Bill Johnson, former mayor of Bethnal Green; James Colthart,
managing director Thomson Newspapers; Tom Keep, militant dockers' leader*

ground that needs all the grace it can get. Far better if you have to play against Leicestershire to do so at Ashby-de-la-Zouch or even Hinckley.

The Grace Road wicket was of the true featherbed variety. As soon as the ball bounced, whatever swing or spin had been imparted by the bowler was neutralised, and batsmen were apt to make tall scores. Against us in 1947, on the first day, Leicestershire made 420 for 9 declared. Our opening bowler, Ray Smith, bowled 56 overs — 55 of them consecutively. (It should be said that he mixed his pace bowling with alleged off-spinners.) Essex replied with 435, of which I made 157, my highest first-class score. Leicestershire in their second innings made 308 for 2 and the match was left drawn when Essex had reached 158 for 5.

Leicestershire had some interesting characters. For many years Les Berry was their Mr Cricket. They had a fine natural bat in Maurice Tompkin, who tragically died in his prime. They had two Australians. One was Vic Jackson, who bowled rather ordinary off-breaks, but these were accompanied by some expressive language and much rolling of the eyes which gave them an extra dimension. The other was Jack Walsh, who bowled leg-breaks and chinamen; when he pitched them on a suitable wicket he was almost unplayable.

The thing that remains strongest in my mind is the particular brand of Leicestershire calling when they were not quite sure of a run. 'Wait back!' the two batsmen would shout at the top of their voices. If I had to give Leicestershire a motto it would be 'Wait back.'

The Ashby-de-la-Zouch ground was as improbable as its name. We stayed at the Royal, changed for the game in our bedrooms, and then walked through the gardens of the hotel and entered the rural cricket ground through a private gate. It was like country-house cricket.

One of our players, Bill Greensmith, had his 21st birthday while we were playing at Ashby. I took it on myself to organise a special dinner party in the hotel, with candles and all. Came the time of the meal — no Bill. Nor could he be found. We feasted without the guest of honour. It appeared no-one had told Bill of our intention and he had gone off to celebrate on his own.

For the last time this summer we leave the northern part of England and travel south to play Surrey at The Oval. This always counted as a home match for Essex.

When we first played at The Oval there were still amateur and professional dressing-rooms, but as the structure of the game changed so did the structure of the Surrey pavilion and they gradually merged.

The Oval has an atmosphere and flavour of its own. Situated just south of the Thames, the ground is surrounded by enormous blocks of flats. As you sit on the players' balcony you look on to the largest first-class cricket ground in England. To the right are the two famous gasometers and behind them in the distance you can see the mother of parliaments and Big Ben. The Oval is Surrey's ground, but much more it is South London's ground.

At one time Surrey seemed to have eleven captains, but all this ended abruptly when Stuart Surridge took over. Stuart was one of the famous family of bat manufacturers of the same name. Their factory was then just down the road from The Oval. He was a large man in every way. He had a large frame, a large heart, he bowled large swingers, and he cracked the whip. Without question he was the boss. He led from the front and gave his orders, reprimands, encouragement and praise in language as spoken in the Borough Market.

This is not to say that the Surrey players stopped chuntering as they batted, bowled, and especially as they fielded; it was that they now had a skipper who understood their chuntering and could orchestrate it and blend it into a harmonious, constructive whole.

The skipper had powerful personalities and players to cope with: Alec Bedser and Eric, Jack Parker, Tony Lock, Jim Laker, Peter May, Peter Loader, to name only a few. He successfully welded them into a team and they won the County Championship five times in a row. It was a remarkable performance and through it all Stuart Surridge remained himself, and his own man, and that was perhaps his secret. He reminded me in many ways of Brian Sellers, who did much the same for Yorkshire in earlier years.

I made quite a lot of runs against Surrey and I could never understand how Alec Bedser used to get so many wickets in Test cricket, since I never found him all that troublesome. I came to the conclusion he may have had several gears in his bowling and perhaps I, and Essex, did not merit his top one.

From Surrey we go south to Sussex. The cricket once more has a seaside setting. Hove, Hastings, Worthing, Eastbourne — Sussex games are always pleasant fixtures.

There were years when Sussex cricket appeared to be in the possession of certain families, and if your name was not Langridge, Oakes, Cox, Parks or Cornford you were a bit of an outsider. It was possible to find a Sussex batting order as follows:

Langridge John
Oakes C.
Parks H.
Langridge Jas.
Cox G.
Oakes J.
Bartlett H.
Nye J.
Cornford W.
Wood J.
Cornford J.

The cricket had an atmosphere of families at the seaside too. The boundaries would be ringed by deckchairs with rugs and thermos flasks and picnic baskets and straw hats.

I enjoyed the Hove ground most. Somehow the pace of the wicket was just right for the lobbing of sixes into the pavilion stand.

One of the best batting wickets in the country is reckoned to be on the Saffrons ground at Eastbourne. We went there once and got 460 in our first innings, with Trevor Bailey getting a double-hundred. Sussex replied with a modest 248 and were required to follow on. In their second innings they got 477 for 6 and the match was drawn. George Cox is shown on the scoresheet as st Wade b Dodds 186. I can't think why George should have succumbed in this way. Perhaps he considered a bowler of my calibre beneath his dignity.

Over the border from Sussex we come to Hampshire. The distance may not be great but the cricket was different. The air of Hove is noted for its bracing quality. At Bournemouth it is soporific. It needed Desmond Eagar, their lively captain and later secretary, to keep the whole thing moving. The other Hampshire grounds we played on were Southampton and Portsmouth. It was not surprising that from so seafaring a centre some of their home-grown players appeared to walk with an inherited nautical gait.

Later Hampshire imported some of the most exciting batsmen in the world like Roy Marshall and Barry Richards, who brightened things up.

Any batsman visiting Hampshire in the 'fifties and 'sixties would have a niggly worry in the back of his mind as to how he was going to handle that great length and seam bowler Derek Shackleton.

I have sometimes heard of this or that bowler who was so accurate he could drop the ball on a sixpence. Derek Shackleton was the nearest I came to seeing a bowler who could do this. And what is more he could go on doing it all day and all summer.

It is now our last away match of the season. We have one player who will not be with us next year — our senior professional, who is retiring. Some of us are sent into the town to purchase a suitable gift to be given from all the players to mark this parting. The presentation is made with a little speech from the captain and a word or two from the player. Cricketers are not much given to sentiment and it is soon and pleasantly done and we go out into the sunlight and on with the game.

Also, because it is the last away game, rather more refreshment than usual is drunk in Hampshire's hospitable tents before leaving the ground, and in the hotel bar after dinner.

The final Essex week is at Clacton and a very good place to end. It is the last week in August. The East Anglian wheatfields are ripe and the harvest is in full swing. The hot sun is tempered by the bracing East-coast breezes. The light is as bright as any found in England and the sky and cloud effects are those that Constable made immortal.

Clacton is a holiday centre and the season is at its height. Butlins Camp is at one end of the town and the cricket ground is at the other. The pitch is in the middle of a recreation ground but it looks nice enough in its setting of marquees.

The railway runs along one boundary and the engine-drivers were apt to back their monsters down from Clacton, and these would puff smoke and blow off steam as the drivers and their mates leant out of their cabs to get a free look at the cricket.

On the other side of the ground were some cornfields. In my first season I had in my cricket bag a shotgun I used in Burma. Its first employment had been by Naga tribesmen chasing the Japanese. One afternoon while my colleagues were batting, I walked over to the cornfields and shot a couple of rabbits. These somehow found their way into the legs of Tom Pearce's trousers. As the rabbits were supporting large numbers of other livestock, it was with considerable anticipation that the team watched their captain change at the end of the day. However, he had the laugh on us by accepting the rabbits as a gift and taking them home for supper. And if he was bitten he never let on.

Essex have never yet had the experience of ending the season with the excitement and glory of winning the County Championship, or even getting near it. Sometimes during my career it was the other way round and we were competing for the wooden spoon.

But we did win one trophy, and perhaps it was the most important one. The *News Chronicle*, then a national daily paper, started a Brighter Cricket competition, with a shield given to the side which scored at the fastest rate throughout the season. With the notable exception of Trevor Bailey, Essex had become a team of dashing batsmen, and we had little difficulty in winning this competition in the two years it was staged. I like to think there was some connection between my obedience to the thought to 'hit the ball hard and enjoy it' and our success.

With the last ball bowled at Clacton the Essex county season was ended but there were still some bits and pieces to come.

A number of us would leave immediately for the Festival weeks in Scarborough and Hastings. After that there would be some one-day matches in Essex in aid of whichever player had a benefit that year.

I myself often played in the Hastings Festival. There were two matches. One was an England XI against whichever overseas side was touring that summer. The other might be the North of England against the South.

It was always an enjoyable week and the match fee was a welcome bonus to one's salary. The professionals stayed at the Castle Hotel and part of the pleasure of this week was the opportunity it gave to get to know the players from other counties in a way that was not possible when playing against them.

The cricket was never very serious. One morning, when my side lost a couple of quick wickets, we had to send someone at the double round to the hotel to get the later batsmen out of bed.

Splendid receptions would be given in the evening. I remember going to one of these when our opponents were the West Indians and observing a shy young man drinking tomato juice and standing by himself. I went over and spoke to him. His name was Garfield

Sobers. This had been his first tour of England.

After Hastings, the summer's end was really near. As you stood in the cricket field of a club like Epping for one of the final one-day matches of the year you could sense the strain of the county round oozing out of you. It was a wonderful relaxing feeling in the stillness and warmth of a late summer's afternoon. You and nature were at one. She, too, had given of her best the summer through. The trees were just beginning to show signs of shedding their first leaves and the yellowing grass along the hedgerows matched the golden stubble of the empty fields. It was a time of fruit-gathering and black-berrying. The swallows had left for their winter quarters and soon, in a day or so, would you.

Cricketers' winter occupations varied considerably. I spent my first two winters based on my father's vicarage in Warwickshire. I kept fit digging the garden and did some work with the then Bishop of Coventry. I was often offered coaching jobs in South Africa and once in Australia, but never felt it right to take them.

The other winters of my cricket career were spent working with Moral Re-Armament, first in London and the industrial areas of Britain, and later in India, Australia, America, and Europe. All work for Moral Re-Armament is done on a voluntary unpaid basis.

Some Essex cricketers were professional footballers, like Frank Rist, Brian Taylor and Gordon Barker. Peter Smith and Sonny Avery had sports shops. Ray Smith and Tom Wade were farmers. Paul Gibb often coached in South Africa, as did other players from time to time. Some took office jobs and one player used to drive new cars from the factory to the showrooms.

So the seasons came and went.

CHAPTER 11

Bouncers

For fourteen years, on summer mornings at 11.30 I would have to walk out and face the fastest bowlers in the land, knowing that periodically they would let go a bouncer, with the purpose of hitting me on the head or body, or trying to frighten me into getting myself out.

A friend I visited in hospital introduced me to a man in a nearby bed who turned out to be Group Captain Leonard Cheshire, VC, the outstandingly courageous man who founded the famous Cheshire Homes for the physically disabled. As soon as Cheshire heard I was a cricketer, he asked me how anyone could possibly have the courage to stand up to fast bowlers like Fred Trueman. I told him my experience in the matter.

I am not a man of great courage. A number of blows on the head had left me with the belief that it was an experience to be avoided if possible and, as I have said, I thought of abandoning batting for bowling to reduce the risk. However, when I surprisingly became an opening batsman in first-class cricket, the problem had to be faced.

A batsman getting a bouncer has three alternatives. He can play it with a dead bat, provided the ball is not too high. He can duck under it, or sway out of its way. Or he can go on the offensive and play the hook shot.

The hook is an exhilarating stroke to play and to see played. Done well, the ball has either to be hit down, or hit so hard that it goes over the boundary for six. A slight error and there is every likelihood of being caught out, or, if one misses and one's head is behind the line of the ball, knocked out.

My brief, to 'hit the ball hard and enjoy it', put me in an immediate dilemma. The fast bowler would pitch the ball up and I would drive it. This would annoy him, so he would drop it short and I would hook. There followed a hectic, ding-dong battle, with all concerned on their toes wondering what was going to happen next — not least me. This merry life is fine provided one has been endowed with nerves of steel. Unfortunately my nerves seemed to have been constructed of some other substance, and I became well acquainted with the sensation known as fear.

I did not know what to do about fear. I knew that one was supposed not to be afraid and that fear was a bad thing. But the reality was that I was afraid. Whenever the heat was on and the wicket dodgy and the balls fast and flying, fear came into my heart.

I longed to be free of fear. I prayed God would take it from me. He didn't seem to. I decided it must be the one thing in my life that God would not remove, like the bodily infirmity that St Paul talked about. St Paul had asked God to take this thing out. When He didn't, Paul came to the conclusion that God's purpose was to let it remain, so that he would stay humble. My fear stayed, and I was much ashamed of it.

I consulted some spiritual advisers. Two whom I much respected gave me the counsel that 'perfect love casts out fear'. It was thoroughbred theology, but so missed my need that I would cheerfully have dotted both with a bouncer had I been able.

Others said that honesty about one's fear was known to help. I tried being honest about mine. In a match against Surrey soon after I got this advice, I would go up to my batting partner every few overs and tell him my fear that the opposition would start letting go the bouncer. I can't imagine what he thought was going on. But the fear failed to disappear.

It seemed to work in a funny way, since no bouncers were bowled. Then, when I had scored 97, Peter Loader let one go. I mishooked, and was caught out. Later I learned that Surrey's captain, Stuart Surridge, had told Loader, who was a new bowler then, that on no account was he to bowl bouncers at me or I would hook the daylights out of him!

Before I came to understand the nature of fear, my daily jousts with fast bowlers continued, with Fear in a ringside seat making his wretched suggestions.

I came near to finding the answer one summer. South Africa were the touring side. They had a fast bowler called Cuan McCarthy. His friends and colleagues called him 'Chuck'. It would appear that some thought his bowling action suspect. Anyway, however he did it, Chuck McCarthy was said to deliver the ball with great velocity.

Essex were due to play the South Africans on the lively wicket at Ilford. I was not relishing the encounter. Fortunately our masseur persuaded Chuck that his ankle was in no shape to bowl on, and he didn't play.

But at the end of the season I was selected to play for the South of England against the South Africans, in the Hastings Cricket Festival. On the morning of the match I rose earlier than usual for my time of 'two-way' prayer. Dominating my mind was the battle with Cuan that lay ahead. I began in my mind's eye ducking the bouncers, trying to play them with a dead bat, or hooking them.

The thought then came to me that I was trying to find some sort of security in technique when in fact there was no security in that direction, but only in my faith in God. I needed to hit the ball hard and enjoy it, and play the most attractive cricket I could for Him, trusting Him with everything else. With this conviction came a great sense of peace which remained so long as it stayed as my dominant thought.

I took strike against McCarthy. He had all his men crouching in a circle around the wicket in what was known as an umbrella field. He started his long run and battle commenced. After two overs he had received such a battering that his umbrella field was now widely scattered. At lunch time he came straight over to me and said, 'Dickie, I would like to say how much I admire the way you play cricket!'

Another summer things had not been going well either for me or for Essex. In most county sides there is one fast bowler and one who is not quite so hostile. There is a temptation, if one is not keen on fast bowling, to stay as much as possible at the less hostile end. If the running of two runs means getting down to that end, then one's judgment always seems to indicate that only a single run is possible. One loudly indicates to one's partner that a second is out of the question. It is an old trick and that summer I had slipped into it.

My opening partner at the time was Gordon Barker. He was much shorter than me, and a ball which might come up to my chest would be in line with his head. So it was even more awkward for him to face the short stuff. He and Brian Taylor were great friends, and Brian used to come in at number three.

We went to play Northants, for whom 'Typhoon' Frank Tyson

was playing, then the fastest bowler in the world. The game was on the ground of my old school, Wellingborough, and it happened that the pitch was so docile that Frank could scarcely get the ball above stump high. But to my surprise I found that first Gordon and then, when he was out, Brian, were intent on keeping me at the receiving end of Tyson; one run was being turned into risky twos. In the end, and in consequence, I was run out.

I was so furious I could gladly have stuck a knife into my two colleagues. I wondered what made me so angry. As I thought about it I realised it was because Gordon and Brian had found me out. My pride was hurt. I talked it over with a friend that evening. He was very matter-of-fact. 'When are you going to be honest with them?' he said. It was the advice I needed but it was the last thing I wanted to do.

I hesitated for two weeks. Then one morning, after breakfast in the hotel where we were staying, I asked Gordon and Brian if I could have a word with them. I told them I realised I had been trying to dodge away from the hostile bowlers, and that I thought they had rumbled this. I then explained what had gone on in my mind during the match against Northants. I said I was a coward by nature, but I had decided never again to dodge facing what I should. Would they help me to keep to that decision? They both laughed. Their response was open-hearted and generous.

An interesting thing happened. For some time the atmosphere in our dressing-room had not been all it should, nor had we been having much success on the field. Now, both the atmosphere and our fortunes changed immediately. Our next match was against Kent. As far as fast bowling went it was an immediate test, for I always had a battle with their opening bowler, Fred Ridgway.

Doug Insole, the Essex skipper at the time, wrote later of this match: 'It was played on a really fast, green wicket against Fred Ridgway, a genuinely quick, thoroughly aggressive bowler. Fred became so incensed at being hooked and cut and slashed by Dickie that he lost control. He bowled shorter and shorter and faster and faster on a pitch that was made for him.' At lunch I think Essex were 159 without loss. We won that match and, in the next game, beat Surrey, then county champions.

Many years later I met Fred Ridgway at Lord's. He came up with a large smile. 'I always hated playing against you,' he said. 'I couldn't bowl at you.'

It was not until near the end of my cricket career that I found the full answer to fear of fast bowling.

In my last season with Essex, I was persuaded by a cautious friend that the time for hooking was over. I was advised that, with advancing age, it was better to duck the bouncer. This was easier said than done. I had never learned to duck. When I tried it against one fast bowler I simply knocked over the wicket, a humiliating performance.

The next year I was invited to play at Lord's for MCC against this same bowler. I knew what to expect. On the morning of the match, however, there came the much-sought-after truth. Fear was a temptation in the same way that lust, greed, or the desire to steal can be a temptation. The temptation itself is not a sin. It only becomes one when given in to. I had always wanted to be free of what I now saw as the temptation of fear. I had drawn no line between the temptation and the act that might follow the temptation. I saw that I might never be free of fear as a temptation, any more than I might ever be free of other temptations. What I needed to do was to recognise the temptation and deal with it.

'Aha!' some might say, 'what if, having recognised it, the temptation is too strong?' My reply would be that this is where God comes in. He has said He will never let us be tempted beyond what we can bear. I know that having recognised my temptation and called it by its right name, I can turn to Him and He will give me the strength I need. The decision is mine.

So I went into this match at Lord's and was strongly tempted. Thoughts of a broken jaw, and teeth lying all over the pitch from a blow in the mouth, were recognised for what they were and immediately dismissed.

The opposing fast bowler knew nothing of this. All he could remember was what had happened the previous year and no doubt he had high hopes of repeating it. He placed his man on the square-leg boundary, and bounced the ball with speed and gusto. Old or not, I never remember hooking balls better. The fielder at deep square leg had scarcely time to move before the balls reached the boundary.

But my best memory is of the Lord's young professionals. Youth does not often look on age with approval. But on this occasion they came out onto their balcony and cheered.

Some time after this I played at Lord's for MCC against a side from Bermuda. Later I met the man who opened the bowling that day. He was a very large man. He told me, 'It was my first time at Lord's. I was big and strong and really fancied myself. I was used to batsmen backing away from me. It was a lovely sunny morning, and I said to myself, ''Today I'll really let them go and show them.'' Then I saw this grey-haired old man come in to open the innings. He hit my first delivery like a bullet for four, so I clapped my hands for the ball and really slipped him my bouncer. Man — he hit it clean out of the ground.'

I often wondered if those who wrote appreciatively at the end of my career realised the battle that had gone on to produce the results they described.

E. M. Wellings in the *Evening News*: 'Dodds . . . played through this age of defensive cricket in a gay, lighthearted, and extremely entertaining manner.'

The Star: 'Men like Dodds are far too rare in big cricket. Yet they are the crowd-pullers who bring in much-needed cash. People come especially to see him bat knowing that whether his innings be long or short it will never be dull. More players like him are the key to bigger attendances at county games.'

Evening Standard: 'Forty minutes of Dodds are easier on the eye than two hours of some batsmen.'

Colin Welch: 'Dickie Dodds opening for Essex, immensely fallible, immensely dashing and entertaining, a beau sabreur, a Cyrano de Bergerac of the Eastern Suburbs.'

A History of Cricket: 'The batting (of Essex) rather reflected the mood of Dodds, who never allowed the new ball to inhibit his strokes. In fact he attacked it from the first over of the innings and by these exciting methods averaged some 1500 runs a year.'

Basil Easterbrook in *Cricket Monthly*: 'From April to mid-September over many years he could not have been happier being just an ordinary member of a team which kept on playing cricket as it was meant to be played long after other clubs adulterated the metal.'

The World of Cricket: 'Dodds retired at the end of the 1959 season after a career which had delighted cricket-followers all over the country.'

I can only say that the Grace of God, when you accept it, is an amazing thing.

CHAPTER 12

An Unusual Benefit

A professional cricketer, if he plays long enough, will be given a 'benefit year' by his county club. When I played, this meant that one three-day county match was set aside, from which he took the proceeds, less the expenses. During his benefit year the player was also entitled to organise other cricket games and money-raising activities. The cash obtained went into a benefit fund which the player received at the end of the year. It was tax-free. The object was to provide the player with capital to start a business or in some other way insure his future when his playing days were ended.

When my turn for a benefit came I did not go first to God about it. My heart was not in Sunday cricket and dances, and the activities of this sort usually connected with benefits, and as I had no alternative ideas, I viewed the whole thing with little enthusiasm. However, there were others in the queue behind me, so I made my application.

The Essex committee granted me 1957 as my benefit year. Following custom, I asked for the Bank Holiday game, normally the best financially. To my surprise, I was told that this was not available, nor, as I recall it, were the next most attractive fixtures. Essex were within their rights over this, but I was furious. That night I drove, with some of my colleagues, down to Bristol where we were to play Gloucestershire. I told them what had happened, and their comments added fuel to my bitterness. I thought I had served the county well and should have been given the game of my choice.

When I awoke the next morning I took my anger and bitterness to God. The following thoughts came: 'You are on the get; your club is on the get; the whole country is on the get. You all need to live on the give. Make your benefit a demonstration of being on the give.'

My bitterness evaporated. I had no idea how this new conception could work out, but I knew now what my intentions were to be. I passed my thoughts on to the Essex secretary. 'Oh well, it's your benefit. You can do with it what you like,' he said.

I looked with new eyes at the matches available. We were to play at Leyton for the first time for many years, and Leyton was in London's East End, where I had a number of friends. It was the area to which I would most have liked to give something. Of the two matches there, the weekend fixture was one of those not available. The other game, against Middlesex, a mid-week one, Essex would allow me to have. Mid-week games are not usually the best financially; on the other hand, I thought, Middlesex was a nearby county with an attractive side, especially if Denis Compton was playing. I decided this was the right match.

Next came the question of whether to insure against rain. To do well out of a benefit match, one needs three fine days, with three days of good cricket, watched by large crowds. If it rains, there is no cricket and no gate money. As the beneficiary has to pay the outgoing expenses of the match, he can actually lose if rain stops play.

I talked it over with an accountant friend, and then turned to God. The thought came: 'If I want you to have the money — I will give you the weather.' So I did not insure. When my Essex team-mates found this out, they were astonished and seemed fascinated to see how it would work out.

When we were playing Yorkshire at Southend, Fred Trueman came up and asked me how much money I expected to get from my benefit. I said I did not think it would be a very large sum. 'Why not?' asked Fred aggressively. I shrank from honestly telling him about not having Sunday matches and so on, because, knowing Fred's reputation and language, I thought he would ridicule such goings-on. So, avoiding a straight answer, I merely said it was because I was having a different sort of benefit. 'You mean because you're not having Sunday matches — I don't blame thee, lad,' said Fred, to my great surprise.

Thereafter I had the chance to get to know Fred, and found, beneath that rough exterior, a warm heart and one that would respond readily to the right thing when he saw it.

1957 was a pretty wet summer. The game before my benefit was against Lancashire at Old Trafford, and there was a lot of rain. After the match, I drove down to Essex with Trevor Bailey. As we sped over the Derbyshire hills, the clouds began to roll away and the sky cleared. The next three days were the finest of the summer; three perfect, sunny days.

If I had been able to say exactly what I wanted to happen in my benefit match, I could not have produced half so good and exciting a game. When I got to the ground on the first morning, and looked at the wicket, my heart sank. It was a typical Essex 'seamer's' wicket.

Essex had a battery of 'seam' bowlers: bowlers who swerve the ball in the air and move it off the wicket, using the seam. The two halves of a cricket ball are sewn together with twine and the seam that results can be used like a rudder, to steer the ball as it travels through the air. If the seam lands on the wicket pointing in one direction or the other, it will move off the wicket in that direction, and it will move in proportion to the degree of purchase the seam makes with the wicket. So if there is a lot of thick, long, juicy, green grass on which the seam can grip, then the movement is very great.

Essex specialised in this sort of pitch. Very good for fast bowlers; dodgy for batsmen. The Essex players took one look at my benefit wicket and said the game would be over in two days. I was tempted to ask to have the grass cut, but the thought came: 'No, leave it as it is.'

The beneficiary in his benefit match has three privileges. He tosses up with the opposing captain for choice of innings; he leads his team out of the pavilion when they take the field; and by ancient custom he is always given a suitable delivery from which to score a run as soon as he goes into bat. This, it is hoped, will save him from the ignominy of a duck on his great day.

I won the toss and we decided to bat. John Warr was the Middlesex opening bowler when Gordon Barker and I went in to start the Essex innings. No self-respecting bowler likes having to bowl a deliberate gift and I could hear John Warr muttering and grumbling to himself as he ran up to offer the usual full toss. However, after this I did not trouble the Middlesex attack for long and was out for nine.

In fact, Essex were all out for 115.

'Poor old Dickie,' some of my colleagues sympathised. That night Middlesex knocked off these runs for the loss of two wickets.

But Denis Compton was not out overnight. There must have

been many in the large crowd on the second morning who came specially to see him bat. He did not disappoint them. He made a magnificent century before lunch — his last hundred but one in first-class cricket. He played some superb shots. I still remember one of them clearly. He ran down the wicket and seemed to be aiming to hit the ball for six over mid-off. At the last moment he turned the angle of his bat and hit it over mid-on for six instead.

Denis was still there at lunch, so many who heard this over the radio may have come in the afternoon to see him continue. However, he was soon dismissed, and Middlesex then collapsed. They led by 159 with a day and a half to go.

By evening Essex had made these runs, with only me out for 48. This meant that, on the third day, we had virtually a single-innings match. Gordon Barker got a hundred, and Insole 93, and we declared our second innings at 377 for 6, leaving Middlesex to get 219 to win. They managed only 144, their last man being dismissed in the dying seconds of the game, amid tremendous excitement.

We had had the three finest days of the summer. We had had three of the biggest mid-week crowds Essex had ever known, with record collections for the beneficiary. And we had had as exciting a cricket match as anyone could wish for, including a century by the most entertaining batsman in the world. I thought of a telegram I received from a friend just before I left for the ground on the first morning of the match. It said, 'My own inadequacy leaves room for His master strokes.' This had been true.

At the end of the game, and before I left the ground, a small boy approached me. I thought he wanted an autograph. Instead, he stood there looking up at me: 'Wot yer going to do wiv all that money, Dick?' he asked.

Truth to tell, I hadn't thought. I found myself saying, 'I'm going to use it to help build a new world.' 'Cor!' he said.

Among those who came to that game were friends from the docks and the East End of London whom I had met through Moral Re-Armament. Some helped to take round the collecting boxes.

For one, it was the last outing of his life. Tod Sloan described himself as a 'watchmaker by trade and an agitator by nature'. He had been a friend of Keir Hardie and Ben Tillet.

I once heard the Bishop of Coventry, Dr Cuthbert Bardsley, describing on the radio the wonders God had wrought in, and through, Tod Sloan's life.

At the time of my benefit match, Tod was nearing the end of it. But he was determined to come to the game. He got out of his sick-bed and put on his best suit and hat. I had him to lunch with some of the players, and he gave them of his best. Two weeks later he died.

Another East End friend to come to the match was Bill Johnson, who had been Mayor of Bethnal Green the previous year. He was a craftsman cabinetmaker and had his workshop in what had once been a stable. Cricket was his first love. And he persuaded the current Mayor of Bethnal Green, a lady, that her duty lay in paying an official visit to my benefit match.

They arrived in the mayoral car and were ushered into the pavilion, where I sat with them. It was soon obvious that cricket was not the Lady Mayor's first love. She stuck it bravely for about half an hour, growing ever more restive. Bill, meanwhile, was lost in the game, absorbing every detail. Finally the mayor turned to Bill and said it was time to be off.

'Certainly,' said Bill, 'we'll just wait till the end of the over.'

Another half hour passed and again the lady remonstrated.

'Yes, yes,' said Bill, 'we'll go just as soon as the over's finished.'

A little while later the mayor turned to him and said, 'Ere, Bill, when's this 'ere over you keep talking about going to end and — wot is an over anyway?'

At the end of the summer, when my benefit fund closed, the sum raised was £2325. I was most grateful to all the people who had worked to raise this money, and to all who had given.

In the first weeks of the autumn I had a growing certainty about the way the money should be used. It had been given to insure my future. With the world in the state it was in, it was my belief that my future, and everyone's, depended on that section of the Lord's Prayer becoming a reality which says, 'Thy will be done on earth as it is in Heaven.'

It was this which Moral Re-Armament was aiming at. I had seen what it had done to bring France and Germany together after the war — statesmen like Schumann and Adenauer said its reconciling work was beyond price — and also its less-publicised solutions in parts of Africa and Asia. I had taken part in some of these adventures during my free winters, and had studied its effectiveness in some of our tough British industrial and race situations as I made the county round. It seemed logical to me that it was the best place to invest for the future.

This was the investment I made. It was customary for a beneficiary to thank all those who had contributed to his benefit by writing a letter, which was printed in the Essex Yearbook. In my letter, I stated how the money was going to be used. The following spring, when the Yearbook was published, several of the national dailies spotted my letter and made a sizable story out of it.

Most of the money went to help work in India. I was especially glad about this since it had been in Asia that I had had my first serious meeting with MRA. It was fitting, too, that I should get a letter of thanks for my gift from my old friend David Watson, who was working there. The *Times of India* wrote: 'A large slice from the proceeds from the benefit match of the Essex opening batsman, T. C. Dickie Dodds, has come to India to be spent on the Moral Re-Armament Movement . . . Dodds has donated the entire money, about Rs 30,000 which, incidentally, comprised all his capital, to help build a new world through the movement.

'Dodds has played several times at the Brabourne Stadium in Bombay. He is widely known in India through his visits to this country and the contribution to "brighter cricket" in England.'

CHAPTER 13

Lord's For All Tastes

For cricket-lovers there is no place quite like Lord's during a Test match. Lord's must be a bit like Heaven. There are many mansions in it. It caters for all tastes, classes, colours, ages, points of view, degrees of skill, levels of knowledge.

It can encompass the Queen. Prime ministers and bishops relax there. A Bradman or a Sobers can display his supreme skill on the pitch, and at lunchtime small boys display their beginnings in the art in impromptu matches on the practice ground, where their rudely struck blows add a spice of danger to the family picnics on the grass.

Long thirsts are slaked at the Tavern bar and, as the day proceeds, so the advice to the players from that most democratic quarter becomes more raucous and explicit.

There are unreserved seats behind the wicket at one end of the ground. The famous pavilion is at the other. It has four tiers. The first is on the level of the pitch. Behind this, in the pavilion proper, and behind glass windows, is the Long Room. In wooden armchairs along these windows sit aged members of MCC guarding themselves against chilling breezes. Standing behind or lounging on the long tables can be found the cricket cognoscenti. Players past and sometimes present, selectors, writers, visitors from far lands on their annual pilgrimage, men (no ladies yet) from many walks of life with one thing in common: allegiance to The Game.

On the floor above the Long Room and between the two players' dressing-rooms at each end of the pavilion is a narrow balcony holding a few hundred spectators. A further flight of stairs leads to the place I like best: the.stand on the pavilion roof. Here, open to sky and sun, one has the entire playing area of Lord's stretched out beneath. And here, if one sits in line with the stumps, can be watched the swerve and spin of the ball and the countering strokes of the bat.

Other diversions are at hand if play is dull. These topmost spectators divide into two groups, with minorities. The main divisions are the talkers and the watchers. The talkers watch as well but are incapable of doing it in silence. They jabber from the moment they arrive until they leave, either at close of play or intermittently to slake overworked throats.

These groups tend to keep apart. For instance, one day I saw actor Trevor Howard, a silent watcher, inadvertently settle himself in the middle of the talkers at the start of a Test match. He cast at first mildly anxious looks around, and then grew more and more exasperated as the verbal flow rolled on until he could stand it no longer and, with a final grunt, collected his belongings and took himself off to quieter parts.

The talkers I like best are the military men. Their conversation is of days of glory long ago. Not glory in military terms — that would never do — but of scrapes old Jumbo got into in some far corner of the world in old colonial days. More up-to-date talk is about the salmon prospects in Scotland, and whether the grouse have nested well and are in plentiful supply. With such conversation tend to go purple-veined complexions.

Among the minorities are the scorers. Some of these statistically minded persons keep not only the score in their books but diagrams of every shot. Then again you will see a radio commentator who has just finished his turn at the microphone and has come to relax and talk to a friend or two, and bask in the sun and general admiration.

But Lord's has many other kingdoms. There are the boxes. With these goes boxmanship. It should be explained that these boxes at Lord's are like those in a theatre. They have perhaps a dozen seats and there is standing room for all who can squeeze themselves within. Of course, it is quite the thing to have a box at Lord's. But they come expensive. The top rate is for those who hire one for the company they work for, or some other commercial interest. Private hire is only half the price. The holder of a box invites his guests to a lavish lunch and liquid refreshment the whole day through. Many are the deals concluded in the most gentlemanly fashion to the sound of ball on willow.

Another quite different atmosphere can be found among the seats that are placed on the grass in front of the enclosures and among those who sit on the grass itself in front of these seats. One day, with my wife and son, I watched a Test match sitting in these seats, just to the left of the pavilion. It was a very pleasant spot in the sun.

We had interesting neighbours. At lunchtime we noticed the man behind us, who was on his own, take out his picnic basket, an elaborate affair. While my small son munched his couple of sandwiches, his eyes widened as this man began with smoked salmon and then removed the plastic cover from a silver dish that contained half a duck, complete with orange salad. This was followed by fruit, and the juice from succulent pears dribbled down his chin before being dealt with by a linen napkin. He finished with some cheese, the whole washed down with a bottle of wine.

On my left, in shirtsleeves in the sun, clearly enjoying themselves, were three men down for the day from the North. My immediate neighbour had a silver flask in his hip-pocket but their main refreshment was from pint glasses of beer that the three of them took turns in replenishing. My neighbour went from time to time to the betting-tent to chance his money on who would do what before lunch and what the score would be at tea. He also had a fine-looking pair of binoculars and I asked him after a while if I could borrow these. This led to conversation.

First it was on the quality of his glasses. But the beer and the contents of his silver flask had inclined him to confidences. He explained the disapproval of his colleagues with his betting on the play. Then he began to probe my own interests. Finally he uncovered my belief in God. 'You're joking,' he said. 'You must be joking.' One thing led to another and I discovered he was a leading psychiatrist in a large northern town, with wide responsibilities. One of his friends was the leading lawyer in the same city. He simply could not believe that in this modern day anyone could really have a simple faith. By the end of the afternoon he had reached the point where his two friends suggested they all forsake the cricket for the bar. He told them to go without him for he 'was having the most interesting conversation of his life.'

To the left and right of the pavilion are the Warner Stand and the Q and Tavern stands which, on Test match and other special days, are filled with Rover ticketholders. Every member of MCC can purchase for each day of a Test two Rover tickets for his friends or relations. And here it is that the MCC member will sit with his family, or park them while he visits the pavilion, where children and women may not go.

There would be no Lord's without the players. Their dressing-
rooms can be easily located. If the spectator looks at the pavilion, he
sees a flagpole at each end. Flying from its head will be the flag of
the team occupying the dressing-room immediately below. On fine
days, especially if their team is doing well, numbers of the players
will be seen sitting on the balcony.

The spectator should not be surprised if one or more of these
players has a pair of binoculars with which he seems to be not so
much following the play as scanning the crowd. Now and then he
will be seen to settle on some particular individual and nudge his
neighbour and point in that direction. This activity is known among
players as 'studying form'. It is usually practised by tailend batsmen
or those who are already out and have time and a mind for dalliance.

When the side occupying the dressng-room is not doing well then
the balcony tends to be less occupied by players. If it is doing really
badly then often all are anxiously watching through the windows
and rapidly getting padded up as they line up for the slaughter.

Many teams have a few dressing-room ground rules. Cricketers
are a superstitious lot. Some firmly believe for instance that if two
batsmen get set then it would break their luck for anyone to move
from the seat or position he is occupying in the dressing-room or
balcony.

Older players who have scored a hundred or taken five wickets
when changing in one position are likely to use those pegs and that
place for the rest of their playing careers.

All players at Lord's have to pass through the Long Room to
reach the field. In doing so they are forced to undergo the close
scrutiny of all its occupants. The fielding side file through in a body.
The batsmen, other than the opening pair, have to do the journey
alone, making their way through the groups of spectators who stop
their chat to peer at him as he gives a final nervous pull on his
batting-gloves before passing from the dark room to the sunlight
beyond to meet his destiny.

Then there is the return trip. A bowler who has taken 5 for 20 is
likely to be given the honour of leading his team from the field and
through the Long Room, where the applause from without will be
continued within, albeit in a restrained and somewhat casual
manner.

A successful batsman will be similarly rewarded. But the

unfortunate fellow who has boobed, and has to retrace his steps after only the briefest stay at the wicket, will have to run the gauntlet of the Long Room amid an awkward silence, stony looks, or averted eyes. As the batsman won't be feeling too good himself he is likely to give as good as he gets before disappearing up the stairs and going through the trauma all cricketers experience on meeting their colleagues after a personal failure to which everyone has been a witness.

I have returned through the Long Room to both treatments. I remember once coming to Lord's and being especially keen to do well. Selectors were said to be present and on the lookout, a circumstance that stirs hope in the heart of the humblest aspirant. I attempted an early hook to a ball that was evidently unhookable, to the delighted surprise of the bowler and the disarray of my stumps. I had negotiated the Long Room and was going up the stairs to our dressing-room when a well-known opera singer on the stairs just ahead of me shouted, not realising I was behind him, to a friend: 'I say, old boy, I've just seen someone get out to the sort of shot I thought only I played on the village green . . . Oh hello, Dickie, I say I didn't see you er, er . . .' But I was gone.

Lord's is a world apart. It is a community, an establishment, a living monument, an atmosphere. One of its treasures is the library over which Mr Green presides, and which contains most of the considerable number of books the game of cricket has inspired.

Within its acres is a shop where cricketana can be bought, and a museum with august relics: bats, yellow with age, which, in the hands of skilled giants of yesteryear, have scored unbelievable numbers of runs on famous occasions, the urn containing the fabled Ashes, cricket boots that encased the feet of the nimble Bradman. In a glass cabinet is a sparrow that was killed by a ball bowled by Jehangir Khan at Tom Pearce, my Essex captain.

Alongside the museum one can wander into another age of a different sort. For here is one of the few real tennis courts. Many a time I have taken friends in there and watched the usually elderly gentlemen playing the game that originated among the monks who played it in the courtyard of their cloisters — hence the word 'court'. The real tennis court still resembles those cloisters of old. The game is courtly too, and complicated beyond my powers to understand.

Lord's has its faithful servants. Its secretaries come and stay a

lifetime, appearing from time to time on television as crises come
and go and call for a spokesman. There are many others less
well-known who have given their lives to keep the wheels of Lord's
running smoothly and seeing to the summer pleasure of countless
thousands. Men like the brothers Dick and Joe Gaby. Dick has
retired and Joe has been there 50 years. Their father was there before
them and started work at Lord's in 1873.

During the Test matches between England and West Indies,
Lord's becomes, in addition to everything else, a test centre for race
relations.

Some years ago I watched part of an England - West Indies match
sitting in the free seats on the popular side. There was a large
number of Caribbean spectators there, together with a good
sprinkling of the 'host community'.

My neighbour, who was heading up the West Indian support, had
made a fine art of spectatorship. He participated in depth. When he
applauded with the help of a motor-hooter with three notes, a
recently-arrived local supporter looked up in surprise, only to have a
cockney neighbour tell him: 'You ain't seen nothing yet mate! E's
got a bell and rattle as well.'

He also had a flagpole with a home-made Caribbean flag atop and
a Union Jack under his seat which he brought out whenever he
thought the home side needed encouragement. His applause would
vary with his assessment of the deed accomplished. A superb cover-
drive for four would see him standing on his seat and having a go
with rattle, bell, and hooter followed by a wave of his flag. When
Sobers got his hundred the flag was taken off its pole and paraded
round the ground like a trooping of the colour.

Things have developed since then. The West Indian Test at
Lord's in 1973, which they handsomely won, was an occasion for
vast celebration. Horns, electric hooters, and whistles, with beer-
cans banged rhythmically together, provided a constant background
of noise. Then when an England wicket fell there would be an
explosion of sound, accompanied by leaps and shrieks and people
doing somersaults on the field. I remember especially a very
muscular West Indian who paraded round the ground naked to the
waist and carrying a large hand-bell. Whenever something of
moment occurred in the favour of the visiting side, he would run
twenty yards out on to the ground, lie on his back, stick his legs
and arms straight up in the air, and vigorously ring the bell for

perhaps a minute before returning behind the boundary.

In the view of many people, including the West Indian Press, the police did a remarkable job in this match. West Indian supporters, in their exuberance, tended to knock off helmets or fling their arms round policemen's necks and kiss them on both cheeks. But they kept their cool and their humour and it paid dividends.

A highly-charged moment came when Boycott was batting and there was a loud appeal for a catch at the wicket, which was turned down. The West Indian supporters were incensed. One of them turned to a policeman and asked him to confirm the injustice. In a flash the bobby, who had patrolled that section of the crowd every day, brushed his leg to indicate that it was Boycott's pad, and not his bat, that the ball had hit. This was accepted. The fact that the policeman had scarcely been watching did not matter. He had now, through his behaviour, established a position of trust and authority on all matters of life, including cricket.

The West Indians and the English enjoy their cricket in different ways. In a free society the problem is how to decide when one man's enjoyment intrudes on that of his neighbour. Those who don't like chat while they watch can move out of earshot to a quieter place. But what of the spectator who brings an electric horn to the game which he sounds twice an over throughout the day, making 28,000 other people listen to it even though it may not be their favourite form of music? And does the spectator voluntarily restrain himself and not run onto the pitch, or does everyone have to be put behind a wire fence?

These problems at Lord's are a microcosm of similar problems being worked out in a hundred communities of mixed races all over Britain. Detached attitudes are maintained in the cool of the pavilion and the smoking-rooms of parliament. But it is in the heat and noise of the popular side at Lord's or the teeming tenements or the bus-stops of Brixton or Bradford that the realities of the mixing of the races and cultures is experienced and a synthesis worked out.

CHAPTER 14

Cricket Extras

On a visit to Guyana, in the Caribbean, Conrad Hunte, the former West Indian opening bat, and I were invited to take part in a special cricket match between two local sides way out in the country.

Conrad was to play for one team and I the other. Conrad's side batted first and he took first ball. I was stationed at forward short leg. The first delivery whistled by Conrad's nose at electronic speed. The next flew by his left ear. I wondered where the next was going and so, I imagine, did he. It was a fast yorker and bowled him.

I am told that the great W. G. Grace, in a similar situation, turned round and replaced the bails and then growled at the bowler, 'What the devil do you think you're playing at? People have come to watch me bat, not you bowl.' And he then continued his innings.

Conrad, however, acknowledged the bowler's success with his usual large-hearted generosity and retired. I was smiling at my luck in being on the same side as this bowler. Our captain seeing my grin asked me if it was on account of our bowler's action. I said I hadn't seen his action. 'Oh,' said the captain, 'many people think it is a bit suspect. We usually overcome the difficulty by having the umpire call him for throwing a couple of times and then letting him continue.'

Next ball I looked over my shoulder as the man charged in on his 30-yard run. This run was a wasted effort for when he reached the wicket all pretence at a legal delivery vanished and he propelled the ball by a method that would have done credit to an American baseball star.

However his throwing arm soon tired and our opponents' batting flourished. The mid-day sun grew hotter and the heat shimmered and rebounded off the hard, baked ground, and dehydrated us as we chased round the field. I began to cast longing looks at the cool water in a canal that ran alongside the boundary.

When the players congregated at the fall of a wicket I asked about the possibility of a swim after the game. They laughed and looked at each other in a knowing and mischievous way.

'It's OK,' said one, 'providing you keep your eyes open for our friends in the deep.'

When I had the chance on the boundary to take a closer look at the water I saw a big log-like object on the surface. It had a wicked, watchful eye and as this caught mine the whole 'log' slowly submerged and vanished into the depths. Alligators!

Before the First World War, Worcestershire had a very promising young batsman called Frank Chester. During the subsequent hostilities he was wounded and lost his right arm — and thereby his capacity to follow the career that had begun with such high hopes. But Frank was a young man of character, and he turned to umpiring. Soon he became one of the best umpires in the country and, finally, was universally acclaimed as the best in the world.

It was easy to recognise Frank Chester on the field. His lean figure was always well and neatly dressed and topped by a trilby hat, and his dummy left hand was encased in a dark leather glove.

Frank stood in my first county game. I sensed his appraising eye on me, as it was on all new players. He was rather like a connoisseur of wine, savouring a new vintage. 'Who's this feller?' he would ask an old player. I am told he would always try and give encouragement to a beginner. At any rate, I seemed to pass his inspecting eye in that first match, and he said some kind words.

Perhaps because, in his playing days, he had made his highest score against Essex (178 not out, including four sixes off opening bowler J. W. H. T. Douglas), he always liked to stand in our home games — especially those at the sea. We enjoyed having him, and were forever trying to catch him out on the field. But you had to get up early to catch Frank. We only once succeeded — or thought we did!

The common or garden trick of coming out after an interval and trying to start to bowl from the same end as the one from which you bowled the last over before the interval never had a hope with Frank. However, one day we thought we had a winner. It was a hot afternoon at Westcliff. The match was in a moribund state. Ray Smith, who was always the moving spirit in these affairs, suggested that sometime in the middle of the afternoon he would run up to

bowl and go right over the bowling crease to the batting crease, as
though he was going to bowl from there. Frank would then call 'no
ball', but Ray would not have released the ball — and at last the
great man would have made a mistake. The moment came. The
signal was given to let us all in on the fun. Ray ran straight past the
wicket and he, and we, were all waiting for Frank's roar. Nothing
happened. Ray finally just had to let the ball go. Had Frank nodded
off, or had some sixth sense told him of our plot? Anyway, when
Ray ran up to bowl his next ball, which was quite legitimate, we
were all startled to hear a raucous 'No ball' come from Umpire
Chester! Although afterwards we claimed we had him, he made a
counter claim. At this distance in time, I think I would declare
Frank the winner.

Frank Chester was a great raconteur, and his best stories were
always about his battles with the 'Orstralians' over what he claimed
were their loud and frequent appeals, coming even, he would
darkly insinuate, from fielders in the covers!

At one time my father had a number of students from Iraq. We
decided to raise our own team from the family, including these
young men and one or two more, to play against the village.

Apart from a little practice on our lawn, this was the first time the
Iraqis had ever played cricket. When we were fielding, one of the
village batsmen smote the ball straight up in the air. It was a
towering blow, and after soaring into the sky it appeared to be
coming down at about short extra cover. One of the Iraqi students
— urged on by the rest of us — stationed himself underneath the
ball and stretched out his hands above his head to the heavens.
Meanwhile the village batsmen were taking a leisurely run as they
watched for the outcome of this developing drama. The ball
gathered velocity. The Iraqi's hands remained aloft and the ball
went clean through them and struck him with a flat, though
resounding, thud on the forehead. We watched horrified, expecting
him to fall slowly like felled timber. But nothing happened. He
merely gave a shake of his head and a blink of his eyes as he looked
round for the missile. Meanwhile the two batsmen had also been
stopped in their tracks by the apparent calamity. They failed, till too
late, to see that the ball had bounced off our friend's head at some
speed straight towards one of the wickets, where it dislodged the
bails, and a most unusual run-out was accomplished.

Each year until he died, Colonel Robert Whitby, late of the Indian

Army, invited me to play for his side against the village of Moulsford in Oxfordshire, where he lived.

The village ground adjoined the old vicarage, the colonel's home. The sides he raised were very varied. One year we had playing for us a bishop who was over ninety and a retired lieutenant-commander, RN. The latter looked as all naval commanders should: tall, lean, with a steady eye and a jutting jaw.

That year there had been a drought for some weeks before the game, and the Moulsford pitch, never very certain, was hard and nobbly. When we batted, a village fast bowler with the aid of this pitch was very successful. But towards the end of our innings we were surprised to see him sitting on the ground, taking off his boots. He gave them to another Moulsford player, who put them on and then prepared to bowl himself.

These seemed to be fast bowlers' boots, for the run the new man took was even longer than his predecessor's. We soon saw why. His first ball shot of the pitch and went straight over the wicketkeeper's head. It was frighteningly fast. The bishop was batting at the time and, mercifully, was soon out, unharmed.

The next man in was the commander. He advanced, unflinching, to the wicket. The first ball hit him a resounding smack on the forearm. It knocked the bat clean out of his hands. If he had been anyone other than a naval commander, I think he would have danced a jig in pain. As it was, he merely stood, silently clutching his injured limb, while the village players gathered round.

After a while he collected his bat, took guard, and faced his adversary again. The next ball missed both him and the wicket. Then we saw the commander drop his bat, slowly turn, and walk off the field, ashen-faced, into the pavilion. He was driven to hospital where an x-ray showed his arm was broken.

The following year, when I arrived on the Moulsford ground, the first thing I did was to go and look at the pitch. I saw with relief that recent rains had dampened its fiery nature. Then I enquired after the man who had borrowed the boots the year before. I was told he had gone to live in Hampshire. The afternoon's sport took on a different prospect.

That year I opened the innings for the colonel's eleven with Brian Boobbyer, and old friend and Oxford cricket Blue. The story he tells is that after twenty minutes he was out for 12 runs, and the score was 90 for one.

Colonel Whitby, old and crippled with arthritis and survivor of two, if not three, heart attacks, would always umpire if he could. He did this sitting on a shooting-stick. Once, after he had got up to give a batsman guard, he sat down a foot or so from the stick. He hit the ground with a tremendous thump. We rushed up, alarmed, but he waved us off, slowly regained his feet, and resumed his duties. Whitby was one of the old school. I do not think we shall see their like again.

I only know of one cricketer who started and finished his brief career without scoring a run. Some years ago I received an unexpected invitation to act as guardian to His Imperial Highness Prince Philip Makonnen, grandson of the late Emperor of Ethiopia. I think it was perhaps as big a stretch for me to take on the job as it was for the 15-year-old prince to accept me as his guardian while he was at school in England. Anyway, we both did the best we could.

I was gratified when shortly after we began our partnership Philip evinced a keen interest in cricket. When holiday studies with a private tutor became too much, an event which occurred with great frequency, he and I would retire to the garden for cricket practice on the lawn. His Highness, though very keen, was not the most natural cricketer in the world. But encouragement was given, and the ball was increasingly struck, and even the glass of our French windows was once comprehensively shattered.

But as any cricketer knows, net-play palls after a while and one longs for the real thing. We had been to Lord's and The Oval and watched the masters at work, and Philip, who never lacked for confidence, was eager to try his hand in the middle.

I arranged for him to join a local club under an anonymous name. They warmly welcomed their new recruit who was so enthusiastic. Philip went to their nets and played in one or two matches before the season ended, but without troubling the scorer.

I myself later played with him twice in scratch elevens against village teams. On the first occasion the captain had been short of a player and my suggestion of Prince Philip was eagerly accepted. Perhaps because Philip failed to make a contribution with the bat, when our captain asked if anyone would keep wicket he immediately volunteered and with such assurance that his offer was taken up and pads and gloves donned before I could get in a warnng. As our bowlers rarely missed the bat the whole thing passed off far better than I dared hope.

One would think that before long a batsman must get a run from a snick through the slips if nothing else — but not with Philip. The second match we played took place in a field from which a fair crop of hay had recently been extracted. The pitch had been arbitrarily selected by the squire in the middle of this meadow and a garden roller, brought down from the Hall, had failed to do more than round off the spikier tips of this Alpine strip.

With the pitch reducing county cricketers and village blacksmith to a common level I thought Philip's moment had arrived. I watched him advance to the crease with the same mixture of hope and apprehension that the whole nation was later to experience as England's batsmen went out to face Lillee and Thomson of Australia. Guard was most professionally taken. The scattered fielders were surveyed. From Philip's stance one would never have guessed the state of his lifetime's average. The bowler ran in, and, wonder of wonders, the ball was struck in the middle of the bat. Philip started to run like a startled stag. But to no avail. The ball was in the air and safely caught. His average remained inviolate.

Shortly after, Prince Philip retired from cricket at the age of seventeen and I don't think he has ever played since.

CHAPTER 15

My Finest Catch

One winter towards the end of my cricket career, I was working in America and was staying on Mackinac Island in the Great Lakes. Usually I am a very sound sleeper, but one night I woke with a strong sense that God had something He wanted to say. I sat up and switched on the light, and the thought came, very clearly, that I was meant to marry a girl called Ann Kerr.

I wrote the thought down, then got out of bed and looked across the lake, shining in bright moonlight. One of the great ore boats from Chicago happened to be passing, and it ploughed quietly by on its way to the St Lawrence Seaway. I got back into bed and was soon asleep.

A few days later I was at an American airport waiting for a delayed passenger. I began to consider the thought that had come in the middle of the night. I did not disapprove of God's selection. Ann was in my view an outstanding English girl and I was strongly attracted. However, I said to God in my heart, 'But I am not in love.'

Immediately the idea came into my mind that if I had married all the girls I thought I had been in love with, I would by now have quite a number of wives. Then I remembered that in many Eastern countries the families decide who marries whom, regardless of feelings. It is in the West that people marry on a basis of being in love. Judging by the number of divorces, it does not seem to work nearly so well as the Eastern custom. Could a third and better way be to let God choose whom we marry, on the grounds that He has a perfect plan for everybody's life?

A week or two later I was again thinking about Ann, and I asked God for a sign. I was by now staying with a very unhappy Canadian family. The father was a prominent minister of religion who was often on the radio and he ran a marriage guidance council. He explained to me that though his own marriage wasn't too good, he was an expert at advising others about theirs. He and his wife had got to the point where, although they lived in the same house, they used to communicate with each other by note. The children were glum and unhappy. The sign I asked from God was that there would be a change in the relationships in that family that very day.

That evening all the family happened to be together after supper. One of the daughters told her parents about all she felt, and apologised for where she had been wrong. This helped break the log-jam of feelings that existed between mother and father, and there were tears and reconciliations that led to a transformation in that family.

The following May we were playing Somerset at Valentines (!) Park in Ilford. It was a hot day, and two Somerset batsmen were set, and were despatching our bowling to all parts of the field. In the middle of the afternoon Bill Greensmith was bowling his leg-breaks, and just as his arm was coming over for one delivery the thought popped into my mind that if a wicket fell that ball, then Ann was definitely the girl I was meant to marry.

To my consternation I saw the ball was one of those that all leg-break bowlers deliver occasionally. The ball slipped out of his fingers and bounced halfway down the wicket. The batsman could have hit it to any part of the field. Instead he hit it straight at me and I caught him out!

But it was not until the following year, 1960, after I had retired from cricket, that the conviction came that the time had come to make a move in Ann's direction. By this time I felt very strongly about her though I had no idea what she felt about me, and I had given her no indication of my feelings.

One summer afternoon as I was watching the closing over of a Test match between England and South Africa on television, Ann came into the room and I proposed to her. I told her of all the events that had led up to this step. Ann was, and looked, very surprised. It seemed I was not someone she had thought of in connection with marriage and that she had, in fact, for some time put the whole idea of marriage out of her mind.

Recently, however, she had had a very vivid dream in which she had been given the choice by God of doing His will or getting married. To her surprise, because marriage was something she had

always wanted, she found herself choosing God's will. Then God
said to her that He was going to give her marriage as well.

Ann and I talked for a long time and then we decided to be quiet
and see what God might have to say. To my surprise Ann's thought
was, 'It's an amazing thing but it feels strangely right.'

So we became engaged. I went to a cupboard where I had hidden
some roses against such an eventuality.

In the next days it was great fun as Ann and I got to know each
other better. We moved step by step as God showed, and never
faster, making plans for our wedding. One day as I was driving past
St Mark's, Kennington, the church near The Oval, I had the
strong conviction that this was where the marriage was meant to be.

My brother Arthur performed the ceremony and Brian
Boobbyer, who played rugby for England and got a double Blue at
Oxford for cricket and rugby, did the double on this occasion by
being best man and giving the address.

When we came out of the church we found television cameras
were waiting. They were greatly interested in Ann's bridesmaids,
for they were a very colourful group. They included an African and
an Africaans girl, a Japanese Olympic diver, the daughter of a
Pakistan general whom I knew when he was an officer in Burma,
and the daughters of two of London's most militant dockers'
leaders. The girls from overseas were dressed in their national
costumes.

Later that day, as Ann and I drove through Essex, we had the
thought to drop in on Mr and Mrs Horace Clark. He had been the
secretary of Essex County Cricket Club for many years and was now
a very sick man. They gave us a tremendous welcome. After tea we
watched the news on their television and were thus able to see, and
share with two old friends, a glimpse of our own wedding.

The years since have been a great unfolding adventure.

I played my last first-class cricket match, against Scotland for
MCC, at Gourock. I was captain of the side. I told Ann as I left that
I might be back in under three days as the Scots were not very good
at cricket. We had quite a strong side including many players from
Kent who were without a county game. The match was finished
well within three days, but it was the Scots who were the winners.
They had the darkest Scotsman I had ever seen bowling for them:
Dr Rudy Webster from Barbados, studying medicine at Edinburgh.
He bowled us out as fast as we came in. One of the Kent players

called him the magician because we could not understand why we kept missing what seemed to be perfectly straight balls.

In 1963 our son Michael George was born. One of my greatest pleasures has been to watch him play cricket. How good a player he will become only time will tell. What is certain is that he loves the game and gets tremendous enjoyment from it. I cannot help comparing the fun and sheer enjoyment I see the boys in Michael's team have in their cricket with what goes on in first-class matches.

As Michael got older Tom Pearce suggested that he should go to Christ's Hospital, where he himself had been to school. He had a presentation to the school which would make this possible, a generous gift that we were glad to accept.

CHAPTER 16

How to Fill Cricket Grounds

From time to time there is a campaign for more cricket coaching in this country. Coaching is fine, and necessary, but teaching the technique of batting, bowling, fielding, and wicketkeeping is only half the battle. To make the instruction complete, the philosophies, aims, and motives of the players should be dealt with as well. These are as important as the mechanics.

For many years Harry Crabtree, with whom I batted a number of times for Essex, was our leading national cricket coach. Now, if my memory serves me right, Harry, who was a very good player and got a lot of runs, did not obtain these by technique alone. He is a Yorkshireman: he has the Yorkshireman's grit. I can recall walking out with Harry to face the opposition and seeing him set his considerable jaw, muttering, 'They're going to have to dig me out today!' When Harry really decided to get runs he most often did. He especially liked to do this against touring sides, as his record shows.

These intangibles, determination and stubbornness, just as much as technique, got Harry his runs.

Someone asked Don Bradman the secret of his phenomenal success. He replied that he treated every ball he got as though it was his first ball — even if he had scored 200.

I was recently coaching a boy of eleven who showed promise. He began to play for his school team. One afternoon he said to me, 'Every time I go in and face my first ball I think, as the bowler is running up, that he's going to bowl me out. Then I say to myself, "No he's not!"'' This seemed to be the beginning of this all-important mental approach.

Very large crowds came to watch the Australians when they came to tour England in 1972. In trying to analyse why they were such an attractive side to watch I came to the conclusion that it was because the aim of their batsmen was to hit the ball and score runs; the aim of their bowlers was to hit the stumps and take wickets; the aim of their side was to win.

If you have one side doing this, the cricket is good. If you have two, I believe the grounds may need enlarging. And all the artificial aids to try and brighten up the game will soon die away.

Many will remember the transformation that came to West Indian cricket in the 'sixties. It began with their tour of Australia in 1960. At the end of that tour I met Conrad Hunte, their opening bat and later vice-captain, who is now one of my closest friends.

He told me that Frank Worrell, their captain in Australia, had laid great stress on teamwork. He said that Worrell quickly diagnosed the character weakness in his team and set out to cure it. There were two main points. The first was cliques. The players from the various West Indian islands tending to stick together. The second was prima donna-ship — players competing against each other to try and prove themselves the star performer.

Worrell told them that if they were to be successful these things had to end. They 'needed to play like a team on the field and live like a family off the field.' He held regular team meetings and encouraged players to discuss openly their problems and difficulties.

The result of Worrell's efforts was startling. West Indies, who had not been notable for their teamwork, suddenly became a united side — and an effective and very popular team. It was estimated that when they left Melbourne at the end of their tour, half-a-million people turned out in the streets to acclaim them.

One year I got interested in tug-of-war as a sport. In the national hundred-stone event at the White City a team from a tiny Sussex village called Russell Green carried all before them against such mighty opposition as Hawker Aircraft, the Metropolitan Police, and Becton Gas.

How did they do it? I called at the home of Mr Pont, 'anchor man' of Russell Green. What was the secret of their success? I asked. 'We're really dedicated here,' said Mr Pont. After a thoughtful pause — and I soon discovered he was given to these pauses — he added, 'Another thing is our team spirit — you have to pull together to do well in tug-of-war.' It was an obvious point so I waited for more as Mr Pont paused again.

Mrs Pont chimed in: 'There's no backbiting,' she said, 'no

talking behind each others' backs. There isn't any malice.'

'Another thing,' said Mr Pont, after a further silence, 'if we lose an end, you'll usually find one of the lads will admit where he went wrong — that his hand went, and so on. There's no blaming the other fellow.'

There was another long pause and I finally asked him if there was any other ingredient in their story of success. 'Well,' he said with a broad grin, 'I really hate losing. I hate losing like hell! There comes a time in every pull when your body wants to stop, when you want to pack it in. It's then I always say to myself, "The other lot probably feel the same — so keep going."'

During my time with Essex there was one philosophical sentence that got me out of trouble on many a day when I was hot and tired or when things were not going right: 'If you point a finger of blame at someone or something else there are three more fingers pointing back at you.'

If I dropped a catch, misfielded a ball, or got out through making a stupid mistake, my first reaction, or anyway very quick second reaction, was to blame someone or something else. The umpire, the wicket, the bumpy outfield, my injured finger.

Then again, if the side was doing badly the batsmen tended to blame the bowlers and vice versa. It often happened in Essex about the end of July, when we were all getting jaded.

The infallible antidote was to look at the three fingers pointing at myself and acknowledge where I was at fault.

The strongest aid to teamwork in my experience is honest apology. I do not mean just the perfunctory apology that a fielder makes up on dropping a catch or a batsman when he returns to the pavilion having hit across a straight half volley — helpful though these things are if they are meant. I think of the more costly apology for things like jealousy, bitterness, and playing for oneself.

For instance, I had a reputation for playing cricket of an entertaining quality. Then one day a young player came along and when I looked out of the dressing-room window to see what all the cheers were about I saw this young man playing with an equal freedom and making glorious strokes. Was I delighted? Was I hell!

Before long I found that although we were on the same side I was hoping he would get out. And the longer he stayed in, and the more brilliant his strokes, the worse I felt. How to deal with it?

The thought came to me that the solution to this was to be

honest with the player concerned and our captain about my jealousy
and say I was sorry. It was not the easiest thing to do, but it took
only a few seconds of time. They both laughed. One said the
obvious thing that if I hadn't mentioned it they would never have
known about it. Both thanked me. But the result was very
interesting. I never felt jealous of this man again and I had a better
relationship with both men than before.

The question is often asked, what is wrong with cricket? Why is
the game so dull and why do the crowds grow smaller? It has often
been written that cricket mirrors the character of those who play it.
If this is true, then a batsman who is driven by purely materialistic
considerations will reflect this in the way he bats, and the resulting
spectacle will be very unsatisfying for those who watch. Materialism
manifestly does not satisfy.

I have often asked players why they play the game. The answers
are illuminating. One of the most prolific acquirers of runs in recent
years put it this way: 'Cricket is my profession. I decided early on I
was going to be a success in it. Success meant runs. What mattered
at the end of the season was how many runs you had scored and
what your average was. I decided I was going to score as many runs
as possible regardless of how I got them.'

It was an honest answer, but I believe this man has been as
responsible as anyone for emptying our grounds. I would not have
crossed the street to watch him bat. Yet I have talked to young
professionals who have said they look on this player as the one they
would most like to copy, because he has been so successful in terms
of career. The success is both selfish and shortsighted if the game
itself is killed.

One year, after a succession of dull University matches between
Oxford and Cambridge before ever-dwindling crowds, I asked the
captain of each side what had been in his mind as he led his team
down the steps of the Lord's pavilion. Both gave the same answer:
'I suppose it was that we must not lose.'

At a first-class cricketer I believed I was meant to provide
recreation for the people who came to watch us play. In our role of
recreation-givers my philosophy was something like this: cricket
should be a creative activity: it is meant to be a reflection of the
greatest Creator: the more the player reflects the nature of the
Creator, the more creative the player becomes. Meanwhile, since all
human beings have within them the capacity to respond to creative

acts, the crowd by their response themselves find recreation.

My battle as I played cricket was always to try and bring myself under God's control: to make not my will but God's operative. The central theme was to hit the ball hard and enjoy it, and play beautiful cricket. It was a humbling experience that the nearer I came to achieving my aim the more I was aware of my inadequacies and imperfections.

My experience is that a change of heart, resulting in a change of aim and motive, can result in cricket being played in a different way. I think there is nothing wrong with the game that a change in the aims and motives of the players would not put right — and quickly. When he was Essex coach, Frank Rist said he looked on Dodds as a miracle man because he changed overnight from being one of the slowest opening bats in the country to one of the fastest.

I believe the sort of cricket and the sort of world we have depends on the choice that the players and all of us make.